WALKING SEASONAL ROADS

WALKING
SEASONAL
ROADS

MARY A. HOOD

Syracuse University Press

Illustrations by Kathleen Lundborg, kslundborg@gmail.com

Copyright © 2012 by Syracuse University Press
Syracuse, New York 13244-5290

All Rights Reserved

First Edition 2012
12 13 14 15 16 17   6 5 4 3 2 1

∞ The paper used in this publication meets the minimum requirements of the American National Standard for Information Sciences—Permanence of Paper for Printed Library Materials, ANSI Z39.48-1992.

For a listing of books published and distributed by Syracuse University Press, visit our Web site at SyracuseUniversityPress.syr.edu.

ISBN: 978-0-8156-0973-5

Library of Congress Cataloging-in-Publication Data

Hood, Mary A., 1944–
    Walking seasonal roads / Mary A. Hood. — 1st ed.
        p. cm.
    Includes bibliographical references.
    ISBN 978-0-8156-0973-5 (cloth : alk. paper) 1. Natural history—New York (State)—Steuben County.   2. Roads—New York (State)—Steuben County. 3. Low-volume roads—New York (State)—Steuben County.   4. Scenic byways— New York (State)—Steuben County.   5. Hood, Mary A., 1944—Travel—New York (State)—Steuben County.   6. Walking—New York (State)—Steuben County. 7. Nature conservation—New York (State)—Steuben County. 8. Steuben County (N.Y.)—Description and travel.   9. Steuben County (N.Y.)—Environmental conditions.   10. Steuben County (N.Y.)—History, Local.   I. Title.
    QH105.N7H66 2012
    912.747'83—dc23   2012006656

Manufactured in the United States of America

This book is in honor of Carolee Prutsman, friend, neighbor, subtle blessing.

Mary A. Hood is the author of *The Strangler Fig and Other Tales: Field Notes of a Conservationist* and *River-Time: Ecotravels on the World's Rivers*. She has published several collections of poetry, general articles on conservation and the environment, and numerous scientific/technical articles in the field of microbial ecology. She is professor emerita at the University of West Florida.

Contents

Illustrations

Acknowledgments

The haikus are by my friend and walking companion, Darleen Abbott.

WALKING SEASONAL ROADS

Introduction

The Road Less Traveled

The seasonal road
Opens to the wanderer
A tale to be told

TO WRITE ABOUT ROADS as a nature writer and an environmentalist might seem paradoxical. The road in American literature has always been a symbol of masculine freedom and adventure. From Walt Whitman's *Song of the Open Road* (1860) to Henry David Thoreau's *Walking* (1862) to Jack Kerouac's *On the Road* (1957) to William Least Heat-Moon's *Blue Highways* (1982), the road has been the way men seek a heroic identity. Yet the reality is that American roads were not created for adventure, meditation, or thinking; they were created for a practical function. American roads were designed and built by a political system to improve commerce and financial gain. That they have been romanticized may reflect that quintessential American characteristic of intertwining the practical with transcendence.

The history of modern U.S. roads might begin in 1896 with two bicycle mechanics from Springfield, Massachusetts, known as the Duryea brothers, who built the first American automobile. From that time on, the automobile, America, and American roads have been entwined like a Gordian knot. Throughout the twentieth century and continuing into the present, vast sums of taxpayers' money have been spent expanding and building roads to accommodate the automobile. Government programs propelled by private industries ensured that the federal government invested in road building. Making the road and the automobile a symbol of America was in the best interest of the automobile manufacturers, and no better example of the relationship between automobile makers and America can be found than in the statement made by Charles E. Wilson, president and CEO of General Motors in 1953. He said, "I thought what was good for our country was good for General Motors and vice versa. The difference did not exist" (Gutfreund 2004, 7).

Under the guise of the Good Roads Movement (Hugill 1981), automobile industrialists lobbied for government funded programs, legislation was enacted, and government agencies were established resulting in a road-based economy and a car culture. The strongest lobby in the country in 1941 was the National Highway Users and its chair was the president of General Motors. Its members included representatives from an enormous number of automobile and transportation-related corporations, such as the Automobile Manufacturers Association, the National Automobile Dealers, American Petroleum Institute, Rubber Manufacturers, American Trucking Association, National Sand and Gravel Association, Portland Cement Association, International Harvester, to list a few (Gutfreund 2004, 33). Some of these groups' most influential actions can be seen in the creation of the first Transcontinental Highway and the Bureau of Public Roads and in the passing of the Highway Federalism Federal Aid Road Act of 1916, the Federal Highway Act of 1921, and Eisenhower's Federal Aid to Highways Act (which established the interstates). In the 1960s and 70s, they were behind the establishment of the Federal Highway Administration (FHWA) and the Department of Transportation (DOT), again, to list a few (Gutfreund 2004). The transportation infrastructure of America, in short, became bound to the automobile, and the companies that made automobiles and had vested interests in automobiles ensured that the government (i.e., the taxpayers) paid for their pathway.

Because of the ease and availability of roads and cars, citizens moved away from congested industrial cities into open lands. And as they did, urban sprawl occurred. The taxpayers' subsidy of automobile transportation resulted in suburbanization, a phenomenon that has reshaped the American landscape. While most economists would argue that the automobile-dependent transportation of the twentieth century has brought great improvements in the quality of American life, it clearly also has created deteriorating center cities, ballooning municipal debt and unstable municipal tax bases, massive development, and fragmentation of the lands (Gutfreund 2004).

Ecologically, roads are not friendly. Roads kill more wildlife than any other force in the country, perhaps as many as a million animals each day on American roads (Braunstein 1996). More than 42,000 humans died from 1999 to 2003 in road accidents (DOT 2005), over half on rural roads (TRIP 2005). The road also has been associated with logging, deforestation, drilling, and all sorts of environmental degradation. The collection entitled, *A Road Runs Through It: Reviving Wild Places* (Petersen 2006), written by some of our foremost environmentalists and nature writers describes the effects of roads on America's wild lands. Yet even if we could separate those intimate partners—the road, the automobile, and the corporations that profit from them—it would be difficult to write about either the roads or the automobile as good or bad. They are both. The road is both killer and connector, fragmenter and uniter, giver and taker.

On a personal level, I know that I would not have the life I do without the car and the road. My mother and father sold Texaco gas, which helped put me through college. My first experience of freedom was driving my daddy's car, for the road has always been a means of traveling and experiencing a wider world. For me, the car and the road were liberators. Every one of us could probably cite similar examples. In today's society, a young person's greatest desire is to own a car because it allows a degree of freedom found nowhere else.

Jannise Ray expresses the paradox of the road when she asks, "How can one hate roads? They are the way we pass through this world, the way we visit each other, the way we connect to place" (Ray 2005, 83). And yet she writes, they are also "contrary to environmental ethics, and all are enemies of wild America" (Ray 2005, 86). So how is it that I would choose the road to tell these stories about place? I believe I have chosen the type of road that is the best metaphor for connector, a type of road that allows for a more mindful way of living. I have chosen the seasonal road, and specifically, the seasonal roads of Steuben County, New York.

Seasonal roads have all the qualities of "the good road." There are not too many of them; they are not excessively costly to maintain; they do not accommodate large numbers of automobiles traveling at high speeds; they are actually more suitable for walking. They are not covered with chip seal or bituminous asphalt or concrete or any of the new synthetic mixtures. They are not coated with dust suppressant or even the environment-friendly soybean oil soapstock. They do not have 15 million tons of salt, the average amount the Environmental Protection Agency (EPA) reports used on today's highways, loaded onto them each year (2009). They have fewer corporate tentacles controlling them.

So what is a seasonal road? It might be best to first say what it is not. It is not the multilane super highway where travel is either the extreme of crawl or the dizzying 85 mph that characterizes every city and town in the United States (and in fact, most every city in the world now). It is not the monotonous interstates lined with corporate chains and clogged with trucks that carry

Walmart junk from one end of the country to the other. It was not the creation of or the handmaiden of corporate America.

Seasonal roads are defined as one-lane dirt roads not maintained during the winter. They generally do not have many houses on them, but they do function as connectors suturing farmers to their fields, neighbors to neighbors, or two more-well-traveled roads to each other. Some are a section of a regularly maintained road. Some serve as access to storage facilities, electrical stations, and communication facilities. Some provide a way to reach hunting lands and camping and recreational areas. Some go through state or public lands and are used to patrol them and keep them safe from illegal activities such as dumping. Some go past cemeteries and allow people to visit and honor their dead. They can be abandoned roadways as people change where they want to go or when towns fade. But always, the seasonal road touches the land in a gentler way.

Their signs read "No maintenance December 1 through April 1," "November 15 through May 1," or "November 15 through April 15," or some other combinations of winter months. They are left alone in winter, perhaps like hibernating animals to rest. And perhaps if we stretch our imaginations, we might imagine them using the solitude of winter to recover.

The term "seasonal road" is probably unique to New York, although other states refer to their dirt and gravel roads in other ways. According to the EPA's *Gravel Roads: Maintenance and Design Manual* (2003), of the four million miles of public roads, two-thirds are gravel or dirt. Wisconsin has what it calls its "rustic roads" (Logan et al. 1995). Minnesota has its limited-use roads. Other states have unpaved roads, gravel roads, low-volume roads, secondary roads, and a variety of other terms to describe them. Generic names include county roads, back roads, and rural roads. Pennsylvania even has a Center for Dirt and Gravel Road Studies at Pennsylvania State University (2011), whose purpose is advocating "the use of environmentally sound principles and strategies where natural systems interact with things manmade." The center describes surface-making aggregates, grade breaks, French mattresses (a way for water to pass under a road through coarse stone), natural stone headwalls and end walls, and all sorts of engineering designs to make the small roads more environmentally friendly.

New York's seasonal roads (also called seasonal limited-use roads) were established in 1975 as Section 205-A of New York Highway Law (New York Highway Law 1975). The New York statutes define what they are legally, that towns are the organizations responsible for them, and how they are to be maintained. In Steuben County, seasonal roads are maintained by its thirty-two townships. The ones I most frequently walked were in the townships of Bath, Howard, Urbana, Avoca, Wheeler, Pulteney, and Prattsburg, although my walking companion and I have traveled nearly every seasonal road in the county.

Why do I choose to walk these roads? The answer is that walking allows access to and an awareness of our environment in a way like no other. Walking slows the thoughts to the pace of meditation and mindfulness. There is probably no other activity that affords us the ease of connecting mind, body, and place. In the words of Rebecca Solnit in *Wanderlust: A History of Walking* (2000, 3), "walking is an amateur act" and "a state in which the mind, the body, and the world are aligned, as though they were three characters finally in conversation together, three notes suddenly making a chord."

Seasonal roads offer advantages over the wilderness trail. A seasonal road generally has a smoother, more even surface, which allows for a safer gait. On many wild trails, obstacles like roots, fallen limbs, and soggy or slippery spots can distract the walker from true contemplation. To spend effort watching every step is not especially conducive to reflection. Seasonal roads offer an easier path to observe the environment, and while the surroundings may not be pristine wilderness (if such places really exist at all), the seasonal roads provide more intimate contact with plants, wildlife, weather events, and people in limited ways—in short, encounters with all of human experiences. As Mary Swander observes in *Out of This World*, "back country roads . . . still evoke an aura of wilderness" (Swander 1995, 206). They let us meet nature in all its healing and restorative powers.

As we begin our walks along the seasonal roads of Steuben County, New York, let me say that each road leads us into places both real and metaphorical. Each road provides an opening into events and issues concerning the environment. Sometimes the road triggers what I know about certain plants and animals; sometimes the road leads into a natural history of a place; sometimes it leads to thoughts on the meaning and the ecology of our lives. The roads offer a means of reflections, and, out of that thinking, an understanding of what is of value and how we might protect it may emerge. Perhaps the roads raise the questions, "In a material world, a world of commerce and practicality, how do we live ethically and responsibly, how do we resolve the conflicts of what we desire and what we need, and can we keep our natural world which is our essential life-affirming connection from disappearing?" Always, the seasonal road opens into a more contemplative place and an enlightened way of being. Join me now in walking the seasonal roads of Steuben County.

1

The Keep and the Hunt

Go and tell the bees
Who live in the weathered shed
It is the old way

CULVER CREEK runs high and loud in early spring. Snow melt rushes down the hills, filling the creek with liquid song. And every time we walk the road, the song is different. One day it might be a lively jig, another day a gulpy didgeridoo, and another a tinkling piano tune—all the different melodies water brings, until summer dries them up. The road follows the creek through a hollow of mostly hardwoods—beech-maple, oak-hickory, and aspen—speckled with stands of hemlock and pine. The hollow is much like that described by Mary Theilgaard Watts (1957, 88): narrow, V-shaped, with north-facing and south-facing slopes that support different "bands of little northerners" as understory.

One spring morning we stood in the road adjusting our binoculars and water bottles getting ready for our walk, when I looked down and around my ankles, honey bees buzzed my socks. I wondered if the bees thought my socks were fuzzy flowers. The bees were from Bonny Hill Honey Farm, and it was good to see them. Bonny Hill Honey Farm is owned by Phillip Glosick, master beekeeper, who I often see selling his honey at the Bath Farmers' Market. I had been reading lately about the disappearance of

bees. The alarming statistics claimed that commercial hives have been declining by more than half since 2006 and that wild honey bees have almost disappeared from the United States. Elizabeth Kolbert (2007) describes some of the theories of where the bees have gone and what might be killing them. When molecular tests were run on the dead bees, she reports, every known bee virus and a multitude of fungi and bacteria were present. The bees' immune systems seemed to have collapsed. "It was as if an insect version of AIDS was sweeping the hives" (53).

Kolbert writes, "the literature of apiculture is vast and seductive; I learned one amazing thing after another" about bees (Kolbert 2007, 52): bees dance to convey the location of food; drones (males) perform no useful function except to mate; races of honey bees have different dispositions—for example, Italians are laid back, Russians are the hardiest; bees suffer from mites and other parasites, bacterial and viral infections, and colony collapse disorder, or CCD. She reports that worldwide there are nearly twenty thousand species of bees and about two dozen species successfully raised by humans, but only one species, the honey bee, *Apis mellifera*, is maintained by North American and European beekeepers. Honey bees were not native to the United States; they were brought over by European settlers. She describes commercial beekeepers and how they transport millions of hives around the country to pollinate various crops. Without these "migrant workers," crops such as almonds, apples, blueberries, cranberries, cherries, cucumbers, pumpkins, watermelons, and cantaloupes would not be produced. She ends the article with a quote from the National Research Council, "pollinator decline is one form of global change that actually does have a credible potential to alter the shape and structure of the terrestrial world."

In *A Keeper of Bees: Notes on Hive and Home*, Allison Wallace (2006) uses bees and the art of beekeeping to illuminate our need for companionship and connection to place. It seems paradoxical, even tragic, that bees, who have been one of humans' longest companions, are declining because of our actions. The use of pesticides wiped out the wild honey bee, our selection of only one bee species to use for crop pollinators has reduced genetic biodiversity, and the way commercial beekeepers handle bees makes them more prone to infections. In short, all these human manipulations have resulted in the bees' decline. What we do always seems to leave some species short.

I remember the first book I read about bees, Sue Hubbell's *A Country Year* (1983) and being intrigued that someone could actually make a living as a beekeeper and honey producer. Her subsequent book, *A Book of Bees: How to Keep Them* (Hubbell 1988), presented a more detailed manual on beekeeping, but it still retained that passion many people seem to have for bees. I also remember being astounded by scientific articles about bees having a dance language and being able to communicate with one another by gyrations (Kirchner and Towne 1994). It is not surprising then that so many nature writers are intrigued by bees and have used them metaphorically in their writings. John Burroughs (1887) calls the bee the honest citizen. Bill McKibben (2006) imagines their "buzzing sound may be the metaphor looking for a place to land" while Barry Lopez (quoted in Garreau 2007) claims bees are a mirror of human culture and wonders if the bee's disappearance serves as a metaphor for the end of the federal government, "the collapse of a piece of machinery like a federal bureaucracy." Diane Ackerman depicts them as "precise timekeepers, who know dandelions and water lilies open at 7:00 a.m., marigolds at 9:00 a.m. and evening primroses not until 6:00 p.m." (Ackerman 2009, 156). She also uses the largely indecipherable journal of L. L. Langstroth, father of American beekeeping, describing it as "the holy grail of beekeepers," to suggest that our diaries and journals are ways of organizing experience and leaving our mark (Ackerman 2009, 162). We have so many ways of seeing bees.

With writings on bees from the how-to-keep manuals to natural histories to folklore to bee biology, it is hard to know where to start. The best current bee biology is probably *The Buzz about Bees: Biology of a Superorganism* by Jurgen Tautz (2008), but others like Douglas Whynot's *Following the Bloom: Across America with the Migratory Beekeepers* (1991) tell interesting stories of how bees are used in our modern-day super-paced agriculture. Tammy Horn in *Bees in America* (2005) presents bee folklore, science, and history and claims we are drawn to bees because their society is a highly structured social system that works. Probably all the authors on bee writings are trying to express the virtues and values of hard work and cooperation. Clearly, there is something about bees that brings out our best intentions.

Beyond the bee range, the road roller-coasters up and down the hollow, then up over the hill and down into Babcock Hollow. The forest is similar to nearby Mossy Bank Park (and the Ted Markham Nature Center), a village park and forest preserve where Dr. Randy Weidner, Jim Peek, and other naturalists give talks and guided nature walks for the community. The white pines whose branches form "platforms like the various levels of a pagoda" (Underhill 2009, 2) offer a hint of sacred scaffolding to the woods, but my favorite trees are the old oaks that line the road. In summer their lush canopy is a green scrim offering shade. In fall and winter, they stand proud and dignified in tattered coats of peeling, flaking bark. Full of holes from prodding woodpeckers and broken limbs from ice storms, their struggle against the wind and the phone book of creatures that feed on and nest in them, is evident by their scars. I like to think of their wounds as medals of valor or plaques for community service. From blue jays to cynipine wasps, the oaks support not only their own kind but also an enormous community of other species (Logan 2005 269, 294). Rarely do we walk the road that we do not see blue jays flying about, in and out of the branches, hurling insults at the crows, and planting acorns to help the trees disperse their seeds, helping the forest replenish itself.

The carved cliffs and exposed rock layers support Christmas ferns that remain green all winter. Evergreen wall hangings, they add the comfort of perpetual chlorophyll to the rock and ice. Below the cliffs at the creek's edge, small patches of trillium bloom for a few short weeks in spring and quickly fade. A red-tailed hawk patrols the field behind the woods and retreats to the quiet pools of creek water and shade in the summer heat. Nuthatches who view the world, "sometimes upside down, sometimes right side up" paint an Audubon portrait with the same colors of the landscape: the bird's "blue and gray are the mists that drift over the meadow, the golden tans on his underside are wisps of dried grass in the meadow, beech leaves in the woods with the sun shining on them or last year's oak leaves that still cling" (Hersey 1967, 31).

One morning I spotted a weasel inking its way across the road, as Marianne Moore (1967, 127) calls its movements, but the image was so brief, I wondered if it was just something floating in my eye. A weasel is such a rare sight, which may explain in part why its name has come to imply a sly and villainous nature. The very word "weasel" means to deceive, but the animal is actually quite straightforward in its cunning and cleverness. Described as the "purest of carnivores" by biologists King and Powell (2006, 3), it is "an effective mouse-harvesting machine." Naturalist Sally Carrighar's description of a mother weasel hunting chipmunks and squirrels for her kits presents a hunter with an extraordinarily keen sense of smell and vision (Carrighar 2002). Helen Hoover claims the weasel "the most beautiful and efficient mousetrap on earth . . . (and) does not deserve its ugly reputation" (Hoover 2003, 253). Unlike the bear or the fox or many of the other woods animals, weasels rarely appear in our stories except as bad characters, an exception being Barry Lopez's tale of the journey and adventures of two young plains Indians, *Crow and Weasel* (Lopez 1990).

Why we label animals in such anthropomorphic ways, I have never quite understood, but one of the great attributes of modern nature writers is that they rewrite some of the old and wrongful images of animals. Annie Dillard, for example, uses an encounter with a weasel to examine her desire to live mindlessly without guile, bias, or motive. She writes "I would like to live as I should . . . like the weasel lives as he should . . . open to time and death painlessly, noticing everything, remembering nothing, choosing the given with a fierce and pointed will" (Dillard 2002, 897). The choice of a weasel to reflect on guilelessness is a clever reversal of thematics. That nature writers choose to do this gives a more truthful and accurate picture of not only a single species of animal but also of the reality of our beautiful and complex world.

Two hunting cabins lie along the road, and about half a mile from Bonny Hill Farm posted signs read "Bath Hunting Club." In mid-November we put on bright orange fluorescent vests whenever we walk because of deer hunting season. I imagine we look like highway construction cones bouncing along the road, but with the number of hunters we encounter, we must be careful not to look like deer. I am always annoyed that I have to dress this way. It bothers me that the woods seem to belong to the hunters this time of year and that I have to accommodate them. But I remind myself that I do not want to be shot. With more and more hunters coming to Steuben County in the last few years, I have a heightened awareness of the dangers of accidents when I walk the back roads.

Coming from a family of hunters, I know about hunting, but have never been especially comfortable with it. As a kid, I liked to hear their stories, just not the killing part. I tried to write one several times, but it never worked. While American literature is full of hunting, from Faulkner (1994) to Hemingway (Hemingway and Hemingway 2003), few have ever had much appeal to me except for Rick Bass's "Her First Elk" (Bass 2006). His story, about a woman who shoots an elk, butchers it, and eats it, is more about connections than killing and death. The hunt becomes a way for the woman to connect to her father. As she skins and cuts up the elk, "it seemed to her that the elk was coming back to life and expanding, even in its diminishment and unloosening" (Bass 2006, 37–38), and when she eats it, the elk becomes part of her.

My unease toward hunting is not unusual. Two collections of essays reflect this irresolution: Pam Houston's *Women on Hunting* (Houston 1994) and David Petersen's *A Hunter's Heart: Honest Essays on Blood Sport* (Petersen 1996). Houston's collection of essays on women and hunting reflects an ambivalence that many women have. About half of the stories and essays are antihunting with the most strident by Alison Baker who presents hunters as vicious, misogynist, and evil, while Susan Griffins presents the radical ecofeminist's dichotomy of male as predator and female as victim. The other writings tend to present various degrees of ambivalence. Even Terry Tempest Williams's essay "Deerskin" expresses the idea that women have never really belonged to that group of men who identify themselves as hunters.

But for all the views, opinions, and thoughts on hunting, it is Jane Kenyon's poem "Deer Season" that reminds me that we humans are carnivores (although not so pure carnivores), and while women, in general, have never been big hunters and men do not need to be hunters any longer, we still need to eat. The act, the art, and the literature of hunting come from that need. Kenyon describes a scene she passes one evening. There are hunters dressed in orange and a farm with lights on in the milking parlor and veal calves are being fattened. She wonders if everything we eat involves a degree of suffering. She resolves the question with, "Moving fast in my car at dusk / I plan our evening meal" (Kenyon 1996, 62).

On Culver Creek Road, I find in the wondrous partnership of the blue jays and oaks, in the close proximity of the trillium and ferns, in all the living that goes on in these woods, a connection that brings a sense of peace. But I am also reminded that like every living creature, I have to eat. Once beekeeping and hunting provided us with sugar and meat, and in practical terms, real sustenance. Today beekeeping is generally either a hobby or part of the agro-industry, and hunting is entertainment. We may not have to keep bees to have sweet foods; we may not have to hunt for protein—but I believe we need that connection to the creatures that share our earth as definitively as we need food.

2

Shunpiking, Whistle Pigs, and Hogweed

Burleson Road

The road lies ahead
From the crest of the hilltop
The road lies behind

WE USUALLY BEGIN walking Burleson Road from Turnpike Road. While strapping on our water bottles and binoculars in this quiet spot, I sometimes imagine the noise and chaos of the old turnpikes. I smell the pungent tar that was once used to lubricate the wheels and said to be so strong that when the air was still, it could be detected all the way to Albany (Palmer 2005). I hear the creaking of the heavy wagons as they groaned up the hills and the teamsters popping their whips to drive the cattle along. Probably the most famous of the New York turnpikes was the Cherry Valley Turnpike, also known as the Third Great Western Turnpike, which included the old Seneca Turnpike and ran through central New York from Albany to Buffalo (now Highway 20) (Nelson 2008). The turnpikes were lined with a string of taverns, one for every mile or two of roads, and the traffic was a never-ending stream of people and goods on the move. From immigrants pushing west to drovers herding livestock to the eastern markets, from stagecoaches carrying passengers and mail to covered wagons

17

and oxcarts (Main 2005), the old turnpikes were busy channels of commerce.

Joe Paddock, a local historian who criss-crossed Steuben County on the back roads for sixty years as a veterinarian, claims this local turnpike was built in 1799. It ran from Bath to Towlesville (about ten miles) and on to Hornell (another ten miles). Tollgates were generally ten miles apart on most turnpikes. Dr. Paddock says that an old house on Gansvoort Street in Bath was a tavern and served as its toll station; the toll station in Towlesville has long since disappeared. About midway from Bath to Towlesville, a distillery occupied a strategic spot. All those purveyors of whiskey made me wonder if liquor played a significant role in the life and times of those early turnpikers. And I wondered whether New York's first temperance association in 1808 (long before most other states) was a result of the abundance of spirits on the roads.

As a turnpike, the road would have been privately financed. Roads at that time were usually owned by a corporation that sold stock subscriptions and paid dividends. While the heyday of the New York turnpike movement was from about 1800 to 1840, there were turnpikes built as early as 1792, and they continued to be built two centuries later (Klein and Majewski 1992). A brief resurgence of plank roads in 1846 ended rather quickly, within about ten years (Klein and Majewski 1994) and all that remains are the namesakes of this road boom. All across the country, roads named "Plank Road" can be found marking the sites of these quirky wooden ways. The canals of the 1820s and then the railroads competed with the turnpikes, followed by the Good Roads Movement at the turn of the century, transforming roads into government-funded projects. All of those factors led to the demise of the turnpike, and by 1845, almost 60 percent of all turnpikes had failed. Thus, the turnpike era came to an end.

The concept of publicly financing highways did not come about until the turn of the twentieth century with the invention of the automobile, and there was much opposition to it. An article in *The Steuben Courier* (1890) entitled "Country Roads" strongly argued against public roads and for keeping them locally built, controlled, and maintained. The argument was made in the context of stopping tax increases. Of course, privately owned roads were not popular either. So the issue of "who pays for our roads" or, for that matter, any public service, seems to have been a source of contention for a long time.

One of the reasons turnpikes failed was the opposition to tolls (Klein and Majewski 1992). Travelers resented tolls going to corporate monopolies. Standard toll rates ran about four cents for a single horse, a sulky, or a one-horse carriage; twelve and a half cents for a wagon with four wheels and two draft animals; and twenty-five cents for a coach or chariot. The only exemptions in 1805 were if a traveler was going to church, to a funeral, to vote, to see a physician or midwife, or to witness in court or military service. Although the penalty was high (five dollars) if caught, toll evasion was rampant. Often there were trails that shortcut through the woods around the toll stations. I imagine that with the availability of liquor, there may have been many incidents of inebriated travelers wandering the woods in an alcoholic haze looking for free passage.

The term "shunpiking" came from the practice of toll evasion. The modern use of "shunpiking" means avoiding major highways to enjoy the less-congested roads, but in the early days, it meant avoiding the payment of tolls. Apparently, human nature has not changed much, because shunpiking (in its original sense) continues today. The Port Authority of New York and New Jersey reported a loss of $7.4 million in 2009 and $6.8 million in 2010 due to toll evasion (Haughney 2011). A trucker named Anthony Foote describes how he avoided tolls (legally, of course). He claimed that if he used the Pennsylvania Turnpike, it would cost him $140, and so he avoided it and took I-80 (Hamill 2007). Because tolls on the New York State Thruway have risen so high in the last few years (about twenty-two cents per mile), truckers have shifted to local roads, causing safety problems and local congestion (*Democrat and Chronicle* 2007). Clearly, no one wants to pay tolls. But who pays for our roads—the public (i.e., the taxpayers) or the users—is still a contentious issue. It seems everyone wants to use roads, but no one wants to pay for them.

Burleson Road is named after one of the first families to settle in the area. It borders corn and hay fields and overlooks a valley that stretches toward the Canisteo River. In the valley below the road, the blacktop Stephens Gulch Road (County 27) is visible. Joshua Stephens, another of the pioneers of the Canisteo Valley, leaves his namesake on that paved road. On the west side of the valley, Spencer Hill, also named for a family of early settlers, is speckled with hillside farms. Like in so many rural areas, the place names come from the early farmers of the region (Vasiliev 2004). The silos, the red barns, and the two-story farmhouses suggest a pastoral strength and stability that may be illusory, because a closer look reveals a sort of shabbiness and a holding-on-by-a-thread quality. Similar to family farms all over the country, they are disappearing or becoming corporate or factory farms; perhaps someday only the names of the farmers will remain on these hills, streams, roads, and landmarks of the area.

One exception is the Palmer Farm, which "milks 190 cows and works 1,300 acres of crops" (Cornell University Cooperative Extension Newsletter 2006). Recognized as a fifteen-year "Dairy of Distinction," it is a beautiful farm, family owned and thriving. I like to imagine it in the same vein as Richard Triumpho's farm in Fulton County. Triumpho's essays *Wait 'Til the Cows Come Home: Farm Country Rambles with a New York Dairyman* are full of beautiful descriptions and pleasures of life on his dairy farm (Truimpho 2005). From pollywogs to his beaver-loving neighbor, Dorothy Richards, his writings capture place and characters of rural New York (a state with a long tradition of outstanding rural writings) like few others.

We walk Burleson more often in early spring and are greeted by shadbushes (*Amelanchier aborea*). Lacy white invitations, they announce the spring party. Their blooms come at the same time the shad fish spawn up the Hudson River, hence the name, shadbush. In the rose family, the small gray-barked trees are also known as June berries or serviceberries, with their flowers turning into berries by June. After the blooms, the berries signaled to the pioneers that the ground had thawed and that it was time to bury the dead or to have the funeral services. To me they signal the beginning of the parade of plants that troop by in all their glory. From coltsfoot to trout lilies, from periwinkles and violets to trillium, from phlox to daisies, from coneflowers to Queen Anne's lace and chicory, from teasel to bull thistle, from touch-me-nots and milkweed to golden rods, the bands of plants march along the roadside to the tune of the ever-changing seasons.

The old shagbark hickories with their loose-plated bark are easy to recognize any time of year. My favorite story about the old trees is one I heard at summer camp. The story goes: A little girl meets an old Indian woman dressed in rags. The woman looks so destitute that when she asks the girl for some food, the little girl gives her a dime, the only money she has. The old woman smiles and slowly walks away down the road. As she waves goodbye to the girl, the old rag woman turns into a shagbark hickory tree. And the girl's generosity is returned each season. In spring, the old tree brings the gift of flowers; in the heat of summer, she provides cool shade; in fall, she offers sweet nuts; and in winter, she gives up her limbs for warm fire.

Birdsong on the road also changes with the seasons. In early summer, the pileated woodpeckers duet in loud arias, but their calls soften in the fall. Crow music is a constant all year. Perennial crooners, they are always full of improvisations and sing-alongs.

Other "meadow music" makers (Chaskey 2005, 98) abound: white-throated sparrows bellow out "Poor Sam Peabody, Peabody, Peabody;" field sparrows ping-pong down stairs; and common yellowthroats repeat their witchy song until their "I beseech you! I beseech you! I beseech you!" (Beebe 1906, 227) becomes as stuck as a broken record. Occasionally, a red-tailed hawk spreads its tail like a hand of face cards, glides overhead, and pierces the air with a jolting screech. The vultures are the anomalies. "Mostly silent birds" (Zacharias 2008, 260), they make no music at all and drift like gliders on silent wings. Birds who "have been so long above it all" (Muldoon 2007, 78), they move through the sky like black silk.

The real noisemakers of the road are the wood frogs. "Frogs being the first creatures on earth to chart the unknown territory of vocal sound" (Levin 1987, 25), they sing in the mode of "all hell breaking loose" (Levin, 27). "Like pebbles clattering in a pail, or a lot of duck quacks" (Kappel-Smith 1979, 248), they are not particularly melodious, but they do get their point across. In the muddy ditches, they lay huge gelatinous egg masses, jelly rolls full of black commas. The commas grow into tadpoles shaped like tiny spoons, and they dart about scooping up larvae and other invisible plankton, the way teenagers search for food. As the pollywogs grow into larger frogs, the vernal pools dry up and their water world shrinks. In that universal reversal that maturing brings, place becomes smaller as the individual grows larger.

In a bend in the road where a copse of trees marks an old cellar hole, shade-loving plants paint a deep green portrait. The old foundation walls are a jigsaw puzzle of gray stones upon which hang vines, lianas, and ferns. In the adjacent sunny meadows, the flutterbys cause the fields to vibrate; duskywings, white admirals, and mourning cloaks all flutter by throughout the summer. When the milkweed matures, monarchs on black-drawn orange wings flitter the days away, touching each blossom in turn as if offering blessings.

We are constantly running into snakes that sun in the road. One day a smooth green snake was bent into a perfect S as if praising the sun by forming its initial. Another time we encountered a black racer coiled on the roadside like a piece of rubber tire. Yet another day an eastern garter snake in a grassy section of the road was so camouflaged we nearly stepped on him. Other reptiles come to the road for sun as well. One spring day, a red eft lay on the road as flat as a cave painting.

Groundhogs are common along the roadside and in the open fields. They pop up, peek around, and disappear. Or sometimes they stand upright immobilized by the sun "like a grandmother . . . her fat belly, her paws resting on her front . . . she seems old and devious" (Stone 2002, 33). "What a type of lazy contentment is the woodchuck," writes William Beebe (1906, 259). These plant-eating rodents may seem languid, but they actually have a considerable repertoire of linguistic skills. Their alarm call, a high-pitched shrill, gives them the name, whistle pigs. They also bark and squeal, make teeth-grinding noises, and chatter. While they do not see especially well, according to naturalist Marcia Bonta, who tells of many close encounters with the woolly creatures (Bonta 1991), they do rely on a keen sense of smell.

My neighbor tells the story of a cousin who came from New York City to visit. She thought the critters were tiny bears and asked why the bears were so small in this part of the country. They do look like little bears and they do hibernate. But unlike bears, groundhogs are true hibernators, and they have been studied as models of biological rhythms and seasonal metabolic cycles. Their circannual clock involves a remarkable series of physiological events in which their body temperature drops from ninety-eight to forty degrees F, their heartbeats fall from eighty-nine to four beats per minute, and their breathing slows to around six breaths a minute (Heinrich 2003). Although they wake up every few weeks to eat and defecate, they maintain this deep metabolic sleep for three or four months (sometimes longer). Hibernation is triggered by an internal clock and is reinforced by daily changes in light known as a photoperiod. Various hormones are produced and the process of adipose deposition occurs—in other words, the rodents make brown fat. What is special about this fat is that it is metabolized for heat—not for energy. A unique protein made during hibernation inhibits the last step in the respiratory chain and instead of making adenosine triphosphate (APT), the energy molecule, the reaction results in heat.

Coming out of hibernation may be a simple wearing off of the hormones. Although large amounts of certain fatty acids seem to be important in the reversal of hibernation, their role is not clear. Sometime around mid- to late February (for males) and late February to mid-March (for females), the animal's metabolism returns to normal and the groundhog begins to feed and look for a mate. Food and sex, it seems, are most creatures' eternal search.

Because groundhogs live at woodland edges, and much of our land has been deforested and cultivated, their populations are not declining. Unlike related species such as prairie dogs, they have not lost their habitat. But because they burrow in crop fields and lawns and because they eat valuable crops, they are considered varmints, and humans spend a lot of time and energy on eradicating them. There are even Web sites that advertise groundhog removal services, with one site listing hundreds of professional groundhog trappers (Professional Wildlife Removal 2007). It never ceases to amaze me what we humans deem pests and seem determined to eradicate. I am reminded of the last line in Maxine Kumin's poem "Woodchucks": "if only they'd all consent to die unseen / gassed underground the quiet Nazi way" (Kumin 1997, 80).

One February 2, we went out to see if any groundhogs were about, hoping for a weather prediction. Groundhog Day is the day halfway between the winter solstice and the vernal equinox and has a long history of being celebrated. As a Christian holiday, it was called Candlemas, and as a pagan holiday, Imbolc (Yoder 2003). Badgers once served the purpose of weather forecaster in medieval Europe, but perhaps because of their vicious nature, they were replaced in the United States, most notably in Punxsutawney, Pennsylvania, by the more docile groundhogs. We saw no groundhogs that day but we did encounter a gang of crows, and in our eagerness to have winter over, we imagined that they did not see their shadows. One has to use whatever tools are available when it comes to helping spring along.

Clearly, the seasons are the clock upon which nature moves. Be it the plants or the animals, the landscape is defined by the seasons. And this is reflected in the literature of the naturalists who write about the land. Every northeastern nature writer has structured his or her writings around the seasons. From Henry David Thoreau to John Burroughs, from Edward Way Teale to Rachel Carson, from Joseph Wood Krutch and Hal Borland to Marcia Bonta, Diane Ackerman and David Carroll, they all have written their compositions to the melodies of the four seasons.

One June, I noticed a small patch of giant hogweed (*Heracleum mantegazzianum*) along the roadside. What a dazzling plant, I thought. But like so many lovely roadside plants, it turns out that this King Kong weed is an invasive (Hyypio and Cope 2006). It comes from the Caucasus Mountains of Asia and was introduced into Europe and North America in the early twentieth century. In New York it was cultivated as an ornamental in Highland Park in Rochester as early as 1917. It escaped gardens and became an "undesirable weed," and like all invasives, its "magnificent ambition [is] to overrun and conquer the surface of the earth" (Maeterlinck 2008, 1). This has resulted in costly state and federal programs designed to root it out.

The plant looks like cow parsnips on steroids. Related to angelica, Queen Anne's lace, carrot, parsley, and hemlock (the shrub, not the tree)—all plants in the Apiaceae family—it gets as tall as a door frame. Its genus name, *Heracleum*, comes from that characteristic. Clusters of white petals as dense as embroidered flowers form the blooms, and the leaves are shaped like corrugated nettle leaves the size of bed pillows.

Hogweed might not be of much concern were it not phytotoxic. The sap contains a glucoside called furocoumarin, which causes skin blisters in susceptible people—in the plant it functions as an insecticide. Although it is compared to poison ivy, hogweed's toxic mechanism is quite different. Poison ivy causes an allergic reaction, the result of exposure to urushiol oil. Considered an autoimmune reaction, urushiol first binds with skin-cell surface proteins; the cells are recognized by T cells as foreign; and the T cells try to kill them. In contrast, the toxic component of hogweed sap, furocoumarin, in the presence of moisture and sunlight is transformed into a chemical that kills skin cells directly by destroying the cell's DNA. Regardless of the mechanism, exposure to hogweed sap can cause serious burns and blindness if it gets into the eyes. In 2003, there were 16,000 cases in Germany, and accounts from Great Britain reported severe reactions in some little kids who were using the long hollow stems for telescopes, peashooters, and play swords (Nice, Johnson, and Bauman 2004).

To eradicate the plant, mechanical removal, obviously, is not suggested; rather glyphosate herbicides such as Roundup are recommended. While I am glad that county extension brochures and articles in the newspaper advise people to beware of the plant's toxic nature, I wonder about the cost of eliminating these "eco-invaders." In New York, the state budget for invasive eradication in 2005–6 was $1 million and in 2007–8 was more than $5 million. I think of all the other services and programs that could be funded with $5 million.

The first year I noticed hogweed, it grew in a small patch about the size of a living room. The next year, it had grown a little more, and the following year it had again expanded its territory. Last year someone bulldozed and plowed under the whole area. I don't know if the hogweed will ever return. Perversely, I find myself wishing that a little might come back. It is a stunningly beautiful plant. But I know that invasives need to be controlled so they do not eliminate the native species.

After walking Burleson, I always feel a little wiser in the ways of the world; the lessons I learn from this seasonal road have to do with basic truths. From the turnpikes, I am reminded that while roads connect us, and everyone wants to use them, someone has to pay the bills. From whistle pigs, I remember that we are creatures of time and the seasons, moved by complex interactions of environment and physiology clocks. And from hogweed, I am reminded that every living organism wants to survive and thrive.

3

Bobolinks Galore

Wearing crowns of gold
They come singing the old songs
Bobolinks are here

WHERE THE ROAD BENDS in a graceful curve, an old clap-board house stands. Its weathered planks, red roof, and yellow-trimmed windows are shaded by a large oak tree. From the old oak hangs a wooden swing. There is a garden with a scarecrow, sometimes clothes on the line, and in fall a hearty woodpile. Everything about the house is solid, and every time I pass the house, I am reminded of my great aunts, Betty, Gertrude, and Anne. They came as immigrants from Wales and lived in a small town in central Wisconsin when I knew them as elderly ladies. Why the house makes me think of those old dears probably has to do with its staid and austere appearance. My great aunts were just that, staid and austere, but generous and kind. What I loved most about them was the way they spoke to me, a child of ten, as if I were a rational and intelligent being, which I was, but almost no one acknowledged that. They also gave me nickels, a great enticement of affection in kids, and never questioned my judgment regarding how I used them. Of course, I used them for ice cream cones, but I sometimes wondered if I should have saved them for something more practical. But alas, the ice cream always won out. And my aunts never once suggested that I be more practical.

One of my recollections of Aunt Anne was a lecture she gave one afternoon over tea on race relations in the South. When I mentioned it to my parents, my father, who was born and raised in Louisiana, got really annoyed and said her take on the situation was "a typical Yankee attitude." Even my mom, who grew up in Wisconsin, was a bit put out and remarked, "I wonder why she doesn't expound on the treatment of the migrant workers around here in her own home?" The Mexican migrant workers picked peas in the nearby fields and lived in squalid camps behind the cannery. My mother's observations made me aware that it is often easier to criticize the injustices that occur elsewhere than to do something about the ones that occur in our own backyard. So one of the lessons I learned visiting those aunts (in this case, more from my mother) was that injustices close to our own life might well be examined before those in distance places. Yet injustices and inequities are probably the same whether they occur in distant places or in our own backyard. And they are maintained by our inability to examine our own culpability and our own inertia.

Some years after I started walking Van Amburg Road, I learned that the house was known as the Woodruff House and that it was the home of Martha and William Treichler. The Treichlers purchased the 1830s house and the eighty-seven-acre farm in 1971 and describe it in *Stories of Mt. Washington* (Treichler and Treichler 2007). Martha writes about living on a dirt road in a collection of poems by that title (Treichler 2011). Proprietors and editors of "a local history magazine for Conhocton, Canisteo, Tioga, Chemung, and the Genesee River Valleys and for the Finger Lakes and Lake Ontario Regions," the Treichlers publish the *Crooked Lake Review*, which contains "the accomplishments of the men, women, and friends who settled in these regions, built houses, cleared farms, and started businesses" (*Crooked Lake Review* 2008).

The Treichlers began the *Crooked Lake Review* in May 1988 and have published 150 issues on the local history of the region. Bill's obituary appears in the 150th issue. In August 2008, the review switched to a blog format.

Described as "the multigenerational homesteading Treichlers" (Kauffman 2006, 81), the family has been organic farmers and remain deeply involved in the decentrist, rural, self-sufficient lifestyle that came out of the Black Mountain movement (Treichler 2004, Black Mountain College Project/Biographies 2004). Four of their five children live clustered around their home, and in keeping with the family's tradition of localism, sustainability, and sound environmental living, their daughter, Rachel Treichler was the Green Party's candidate for New York State Attorney General in 2006 (Treichler 2006, 2008).

I first met Rachel at a Sierra Club meeting, and she has become a local hero of mine. Rachel's wisdom and environmental activism through the Steuben Greens, the Sierra Club Finger Lakes Group, the Finger Lakes Progressives, and the Bath Peace and Justice Group is the kind of action born of courage and hard work. Her accomplishments through these local groups, which I think of as fighting the inertia in her own backyard, have resulted in a county and a region where environmental activism has made a difference (see Scorecard: The Pollution Information Site 2005). Her environmental activism is part of a larger commitment to community as is her online bookstore, EcoBooks (EcoBooks 2008).

Occasionally I meet Rachel on the road, and it's always a joyful encounter. One April morning when the alder catkins were barely fuzzed and the day had that temporary texture of early spring, Rachel came walking up over the hill. I asked about her father, and the topic of conversation turned to some of the old people we knew who were "not long for this world." I remarked that I shouldn't put off talking with some of these folks, and we laughed. Here in that glorious moment of spring with birdsong all around, with wildflowers beginning to bloom, when the whole world seemed determined to resurrect, we were laughing at death in a respectful way. Kathleen Dean Moore writes that we would do well to live life with "gladness and gratitude" (Moore 2004), and I think she might have included that a respectful awareness of death, even in spring, is a good thing.

Van Amburg runs along the ridge of Mt. Washington and overlooks two valleys. On a section that opens into meadows and sky, Keuka Lake is a swatch of blue to the north with Bully Hill Winery breaking the pattern of sloping vineyards and woods. To the south, Birdseye Hollow Lake is a thin sliver of water that changes color to match the sky. The road traverses mixed hardwood forests and hay fields. The open fields, some recently planted in evergreens, bordered with gray dogwood, sumac, and hawthorn give the appearance of a grassland prairie. In fall the shrubs hedge the road in rusty reds and maroons.

Every spring beginning in April, we walk the road in anticipation of bobolinks. Their first sighting, usually not until the first of May, is cause for celebration. The flash of black and white as they rise from the grasses reflects their old common name, skunk bird. The male's bright yellow cap when he sits like a monk on the wire, or when he hovers over the grass, or when he lands on a tiny blade of grass and sways for a moment before disappearing into the grass are sights that clearly mark the beginning of the warm season. But it is the bird's bubbly song that is the most joyous. Its tonal chattering, its dips and crescendos that sound like several birds singing together remind me of ventriloquists who entertain with trickster voices.

We are not the only ones who relish these meadowland birds and take delight in their return. American poets have long been inspired by their appearance. Emily Dickinson wrote three poems about bobolinks, calling them "The Rowdy of the Meadow" and "The Presbyterian birds" (Liebmann 2008). William Cullen Bryant calls them "Robert of Lincoln" (Bryant 1800) and describes them as "merrily swinging on brier and weed." American naturalist John Burroughs (1906) proclaims the bird in his poem "Bobolink," "The gladdest bird that sings and flies." Diane Kappel-Smith writes of the bobolink, "dancing clown of the hay meadow, with his white-gold cape and his nasal poetry" (Kappel-Smith 1979, 10). Likewise, there is probably no American naturalist who has not written something on the bobolink.

Yet for all the admiration of poets and naturalists, bobolinks have not had an easy time. In the last thirty to forty years, bobolinks like many grassland birds have suffered rapid population declines due to habitat loss. The birds breed in the grasslands in North America and winter in the grasslands of South America, so any disruption of those habitats or ones along their route can have an impact on them. Their 12,500-mile round-trip flight every year is a marathon. They leave Brazil, Paraguay, and northern Argentina in March and arrive in Colombia and Venezuela in late April. They cross the Caribbean and the Gulf of Mexico landing in Florida, Louisiana, and Texas. From there they fan out and move northward arriving at their breeding grounds throughout the Midwest and Northeast in May. They breed, raise their young, and by early July, return to spend November through March in South America (Martin and Gavin 1995). The bird's home on two continents and its travels from one to the other shows the extent of its enormous territory.

In the early part of the century, bobolinks were more abundant. Huge flocks would descend on the rice fields of the southeastern United States, and the birds could fatten up for the remainder of the trip. Rice birds, as they were called, were shot and killed by the thousands (Deinlein 1997). Today, one reason for population decline is the earlier and more frequent mowing of hay fields. The cutting of hay occurs two to three weeks earlier than it did fifty years ago and overlaps with the birds' nesting season. In South America, farmers kill the birds outright thinking they are crop-eating pests. Studies and efforts by conservationists (Renfrew 2008) have promoted delaying cutting until July 15, leaving twenty-acre or larger patches of field with a little woody edge uncut and educating farmers to understand that the birds are beneficial as weed-seed and insect eaters.

We look for meadowlarks as well, but each year we see fewer and fewer. Like the bobolink, their populations are also declining. In their black bibs and yellow breasts, to my mind, they bring the sweetest music. Their calls ring out like conversations of flutes. Other birds that also make their home along Van Amburg include the redwing blackbirds. Birds whose numbers never seem to decline, they come in like noisy relatives. Tree swallows also zoom in and perch on the wires and on the bluebird boxes, dressed as if attending a black-tie affair. In their dark tuxedos, bright white fronts, and deeply iridescent blue-green tails, they form a formal receiving line. Later, the towhees arrive and shriek for hours like bagpipes tuning, never seeming to find the right pitch. A bit earlier, yellow warblers puff out their red-streaked breast and blast out their Ethel Merman songs to each other, while common yellowthroats try to compete from the thickets. These are the quintessential birdsongs of summer.

White-tailed deer bounce across the road and disappear into the woods. Of course, there are no longer wolves to prey on the deer. But there once were. In *Stories of Mt. Washington*, the Treichlers recount an old tale: "When the snow was deep and sometimes drifted as high as the eaves of the cabin, the wolves mounted the roofs and would come down the chimney if there were no fires to scare them away. It was then the task of the boys to keep plenty of wood on hand, and keep the fires blazing both night and day." (Treichler and Treichler 2007, 8, 9). I wonder if there was a boy named Peter and if he might have cried "Wolf" or a young boy who could have written like Dylan Thomas (1954):

Years and years and years ago, when I was a boy, when there were wolves in Wales, and birds the color of red-flannel petticoats whisked past the harp-shaped hill, when we sang and wallowed all night and day in caves that smelt like Sunday afternoons in damp front farmhouse parlors, and we chased, with the jawbones of deacons, the English and the bears, before the motor car, before the wheel, before the duchess-faced horse, when we rode the draft and happy hills bareback, it snowed and it snowed.

In the woods beneath the old maples, mayapples open their green umbrellas above the heads of barren strawberries. Woodland accessories, they add a touch of frill to the variegated shade of spring. Clover, birdsfoot trefoil, chicory, wild parsnip, Queen Anne's lace and sensitive fern trim the edges of the open road in lace. Such finery brings to the summer road an elegance and grace. One August, stopping by some raspberry bushes to pick the ripe red berries, a ribbon snake, curled like an ebony necklace, looked me straight in the eye as I reached into the brambles. The snake gave no indication that I had disturbed it at all, but I withdrew my hand carefully. I always like to maintain a certain distance from snakes no matter how innocuous they are. Along the more open sections of road that border the hay fields, gnarly old apple trees live out their waning years in an annual cycle of leaf out, blossom, green fruit, red fruit, fallen fruit, leaf fall, and finally, bare branches etching the sky. Although the trees are aged and worn, the apples are still sweet and juicy. In November they are transformed into Thoreau's wild apples, gnawed by frost, tasting as if they were "baked in ice" (Underhill 2009, 138). By December, the remaining apples have withered to leathery bulbs.

Of all the roads we walk, Van Amburg offers me the strongest sense of comfort and hope. I think the reason might be because of who lives there—the Treichlers and the bobolinks—and I wonder if what they share in common has to do with the love of place. Why else would a family live on this cold windy ridge road for forty years; why else would the bobolinks return year after year traveling thousands and thousands of miles, if they did not love this place and think of it as their beloved home? Perhaps it is the love of place that rings out on this road and that gives the road its hopefulness. My great aunts made their home a place of welcome and comfort, and I found love and understanding there. If we take hope from anything, perhaps it is from those places we call home.

4

Trout Lilies and Trillium

Hungry Hollow Road

In tandem they come
Trout lilies then trillium
Before the spring hum

ONE FALL MORNING a squeal from a culvert caused me to pause and walk over to check it out. To my surprise an enormous raccoon emerged from the creek, shook herself, made a growl of disapproval because she had been disturbed, and waddled off up the hill. Her paws were wet and muddy. Her thick amble reminded me of a bag lady who might have been driven away from her favorite corner, and I apologized to her back. She could have been catching frogs or snails or dousing her food. With winter coming on, I suspect she was making a last-ditch effort to fatten up. A. K. Dewdney describes a raccoon he calls Lotor (after the genus name for the raccoon) as "the chief intellect of Hungry Hollow" (Dewdney 1998, 197) because of her remarkable memory, planning, imagination, and emotional abilities. In his creation of a composite place, Dewdney writes "Hungry Hollow is nowhere and everywhere" (Dewdney 1998, ix). Portraying a place that represents all the eastern deciduous forest regions of North America, his descriptions are thorough and insightful. But this Hungry Hollow is a real place, and the road that runs through it braids around Hungry Hollow Creek in the state forest known as Pigtail Hollow.

The name "Hungry Hollow" dates back to the Depression and probably refers to the poor soil of the area. A farmer might go mighty hungry trying to farm this land (NYSDEC 20011i). But to me it was one of the richest roads we walk, and it offers wonders all year round, especially in spring. What brings these riches is the creek, and the road's minstrel tagalong has a song for every season. In winter its music is muted and frozen, but when spring thaws come, it roars down the hollow. Cascading over thousands of slate stair-steps, tumbling from one to the next, the waterfalls carve potholes, ripples, and scallops in the rocks. In summer the tempo slows and the songs become raspy and weak. In fall the creek readies itself again for the long, cold quiet.

The creek is clearly the artist that has carved the hollow as well as the gardener who maintains it. In some spots the hollow is several hundred feet wide; in others, only a little wider than the road and creek. Where it narrows and takes on the appearance of a gorge, ferns and moss deck the shale walls. It could be a landscape painting from the Hudson River School, maybe similar to James Hope's *Rainbow Falls*. Lush green and almost tropical in summer, the colors shift to the red, yellow, and purple spectrum of the rainbow in fall.

Because of the wildflowers, Hungry Hollow is my favorite road at winter's end. Under a trellised roof among the fluted tree trunks, puddles of wildflowers paint the forest floor. The lower part of the road abounds in April with early meadowrue (*Thalictrum dioicum*). In the buttercup family, the plant grows best in the shade of oak and aspen. It crawls out of the ground purple and wrinkled like a newborn, and unfurls its green leaves to resemble maidenhair fern. Coin-shaped and spaciously arranged, the leaves create airy mobiles. The small hanging flowers that bloom in May produce droopy seeds, and when they wilt, the plant becomes a brown lacy collar accenting the road.

The first flowers to emerge are the coltsfoot (*Tussilago farfara*) known as coughwort. Nonnatives from Europe and Asia, they settle in like dandelions. In fact, they mightily resemble dandelions. They rise from the cold ground gray and stemmy, produce yellow-disk flowers, and bend over like candy canes. Only after the seed is set and the flower has turned to fuzz do they produce leaves. Their crooks and dandy flowers bring the first bright color to the winter road.

Next to appear are the trout lilies (*Erythronium americana*), also called dog's tooth violet or adder's tongue. These colonial natives emerge as two mottled leaves the shape and color of brook trout, and yellow lilies soon arise from the camouflage. The lilies last a couple of weeks and then the plants disappear completely as if the effort of being ahead of the pack was too much to sustain. Only older plants, three or more years, produce flowers. And what delicious lilies they are "nodding in the chequered sunshine of the trees" (Lowell 1912, 37). Opening in daylight, the petals flare back and close at night. Pollinated by ants that eat the nutritious appendages attached to each seed, the plant is rarely propagated by seeds but through an underground root or rhizome system. Thus, the plants are found in colonies, and these colonies can be several hundred years old. In their centenarian congregations, these yellow ground-stars are the best antidote to winter gray. Like so many of the herbaceous plants of the deciduous forest, the trout lily was used by Native Americans for its pharmacological properties, and recently an anticancer compound called alpha-methylene-gamma-butyrolactone has been discovered in the plant.

Trout lilies herald the trilliums. And oh, what lovely triplets they bring! With their green triumvirate leaves and tripetal flowers, they arrive like an inauguration. John Burroughs wrote of trilliums in *Wake-Robin* "and when I have found the wake robin in bloom I know the season is fairly inaugurated. With me this flower is associated, not merely with the awakening of Robin . . . but the universal awakening and rehabilitation of nature" (Burroughs 1871). That poets and naturalists have been especially enamored with these ephemerals is evident by the many inspired flowery phrases. Descriptions like those from poet, A. M. Klein who writes, "upon the easy threes of trillium, dark green, green, white, / threaded with earth, and rooted" (Klein 1990), or those of Josephine Johnson who writes, "wax petals . . . coiled and sailing as the coifs of Belgian nuns. Some curved and seeking, like the necks of swans" (Johnson 1969, 68), clearly illustrate this fascination. But it is Robert Michael Pyle who explains it so succinctly, "Nothing among the wild flora speaks to me of redemption of spring like trilliums" (Pyle 2007, 60).

In the lily family, trilliums have three petals, three sepals, and three leaves; they do seem determined to embody a trinity. The two species we see along the creek are the purples (*Trillium erectum*) followed by the great whites (*T. grandiflorum*). Similar to trout lilies, only the older plants, in this case, seven to ten years old, produce a flower. The best habitats are moist soils beneath beech and maples, and the plants are reported to be a favorite food of white-tailed deer who can consume eight pounds a day. Of the thirty-eight species of *Trillium* in North America and five or six in New York state, the whites are the showiest of the spring flowers, but it is the purple trillium that provide a bit of floral irony. Known as stinking Benjamin, they emit such an unpleasant, rotting-flesh scent (designed to attract carrion flies) that their visual message of resurrection might get muted by the odor of death and decay. But then what is resurrection without its mix of death and dying.

Near the patches of trillium, garlic mustard (*Alliaria petiolata*) intrudes. This nuisance plant grows tall, thin, and white-tipped in early summer and dies back in midsummer, leaving black seeds to ensure its return. While I like the smell of its crushed leaves, the patches get denser and larger every year. The problem with any invasive is that it makes life miserable for native species; garlic mustard is no exception and has been shown to suppress the beneficial mycorrhizal fungi of trillium (Burke 2008) and some native trees (Stinson, et al. 2006), so I pull it whenever I remember. That is, of course, an endless task.

Another native lily, Canada mayflowers (*Maianthemum canadense*), also sprout in patches along the creek. Called false lilies-of-the-valley, these May flowers with their succulent leaves and white fuzzy spiked flowers produce deep red berries by summer's end and join the ever-growing chorus of native perennials. In the shade of the woods, jack-in-the-pulpit (*Arisaema triphyllum*) "preaching to a congregation of thicket dwellers" (Bonta 1991, 126) is the sequential hermaphrodite of the hollow. Wild ginger (*Asarum canadense*) with its toxic aristolochic acid and wild columbines (*Aquilegia canadensis*) like tiny Japanese lanterns light up the roadside.

The nonflowering plants of the hollow are as fascinating as the flowering ones. The club mosses and horsetail ferns, the pteridophytes, like their fern relatives, reproduce not by seeds but by spores. Such prehistoric life-forms, they make me think of dinosaurs and pterodactyls. The lycopods, or the club mosses, are miniature evergreens and might be part of the shrunken world of *Alice in Wonderland* after she drinks from the magical "Drink Me" bottle. The most common species, running ground pine (*Lycopodium obscurum*) rises from the leaf litter like a forest of tiny pine trees, and ground cedar (*L. tristachyum*) grows like bonsai cedars. The horsetail ferns (there are nine species of *Equisetum* common to the region) sprout like green segmented pencils and stand as straight as military cadets. Oliver Sacks describes discovering giant horsetail ferns on a field trip that he and a band of fern enthusiasts take to Mexico. He tells how the nineteenth-century botanist Richard Spruce came upon a primeval forest of them in Ecuador (Sacks 2002, 145). Thick as his waist and fifteen feet tall, they made an alien forest. Clearly, there is something exotic about horsetail ferns, even these familiar species here in Hungry Hollow that are only a few feet tall. The plants seem to stir the imagination, and when I see them, I imagine just for an instant a wild and ancient world that preceded this tame and familiar deciduous Northeast forest.

A horse chestnut tree marks the border of the state forest. It takes so long for the leaves to mature, but finally by midsummer, they expand to the size of ceiling fans, and when it's hot and humid, that curve in the road is the coolest spot. Every September, like Roger Swain, I pick up a pocketful of nuts, those wonderful "oiled and polished mahogany" talismans (Swain 1991, 3) that end up being thrown out after a while. Like Swain I don't know why I pick them up either, but I seem to need the feel of the smooth charms in my pockets.

One spring morning I watched a northern short-tailed shrew grubbing the mud banks for earthworms. In what kind of world do these fossorial creatures live, I wondered. Little furry keychain toys, whose homes are elaborate leaf and snow tunnels, do they have no concept of sky except as the place from which the deadly owls come? And how is it that such diverse creatures—bats of the sky, whales of the oceans, and shrews of the earth—use echolocation to illuminate their dark world? Wallace (1980, 17–20) describes the poison these shrews produce as similar to cobra venom and how their metabolism is so high, they often die of fright. They evoke such a feeling of vulnerability that it is difficult to view them in any other way except with great affection.

The trees along most of the road are hardwoods, typical of oak-hickory and maple-beech forests. The white oaks are the most common with leaves that unfold to "clothe the tree in a veil of vivid red gradually turning pink and then silvery white. In autumn this foliage is a rich winey color." (Peattie 1950, 196). King of the oaks, they are the ones that create the strongest sense of forest here, but the beech with their Midas touch or as Linda Underhill describes their autumn leaves, "gold coins" that create "a rich yellow rain drenching the woods" (Underhill 2009, 85) along with the hickories and their variety of nuts, add Kodachrome to the forest mosaic. The red maples, though, are the showiest, for they offer something red all year round: red buds, red flowers, young red leaves, summer leaf stalks, and the most vivid of all, in fall, the dying leaves (Peattie 1950, 465). Also making their presence known among the oaks, beeches, hickories, and maples, are a few elms, willows, white sycamores, hemlocks, and pines. Occasionally, a wolf tree alters the pattern of these youthful and middle-aged congregations (there are few really old trees in this forest). It is in these old wolf trees with their broad crown and expansive branches that we sometimes see scarlet tanagers, chestnut-sided warblers, and red-eyed vireos.

The forests of the region have always inspired awe. One of the earliest descriptions by settlers in the 1850s illustrates the beauty of this great forest wilderness. "It is a vast solitude, with scarce a sound to break the reigning silence but the splashing of the brooks in their defiles . . . or perhaps the creaking of sulky old hemlocks as the light wind stirs their branches or sways their tottering trunks slowly to and fro" (McMaster 1853).

Near the top of the hill before the road bends into Dinehart Crossing, a grove of birch alters the oak-hickory-maple-beech pattern. In winter they "looked like the desiccated ribs of some enormous beast whose flesh had melted away in the rain" (Klinkenborg 2003, 70). One late summer I noticed small square holes evenly spaced in a partial line ringing the trunk. Did someone chisel a braille tree? No, they were sap wells made by a yellow-bellied sapsucker. The name of this bird always makes me smile. I imagine Gabby Hayes hurling it as an insult at some cowboy villain.

"You dirty rotten yellow-bellied sapsucker!" But the bird is certainly not a villain. The holes the birds drill are called sap licks, and they extract the tree phloem much like we would milk sugar maples. Heinrich (1997, 179) explains that these birds are keystone species and their chisels provide nest holes for other birds and a source of food for many other animals.

Near the birch trees, in fall, a grove of tamaracks stands like "giant candle flames" (Borland 1957, 206). But the tamarack's entire seasonal wardrobe is glorious. Its spring cashmere sweater of yellow-green turns silky green. Inch-long needles catch the wind, and the trees whisper and sigh all summer long. In fall their orange ruffles embroidered with brown roses change to austere gray business suits, as if "it's time to get down to the business of winter." When the hard November winds come, the needles fly off like darts, leaving the tree limbs bare, the color of pin-striped.

White-breasted nuthatches and chickadees flitter in and out of the trees all year round, so the grove is almost always active and noisy. The tree-creeping nuthatch who "spends its time grooming trees" (Gooch 1950, 110) can wedge a nut between the bark and hatchet it with its bill. Black-capped chickadees are little toughies, their commitment to winter undaunted. Not for them the sunny south. All winter, their black-and-white frenetics animate the still winter landscape. These birds play the role of town crier, and their repertoire of more than 360 calls contains an amazing amount of information (Hess 2007). They often form the nucleus of multispecies flocks and attract other types of birds. Collectively, the birds can effectively harass any predators. At least ten other species participate in mobbing when they hear the chickadee's alarm calls. Experiments have shown that when red-breasted nuthatches hear certain chickadee calls, they can distinguish high-threat or low-threat predators. Whether the chickadees are multilingual or the nuthatches and other birds are bilingual, I suppose it doesn't matter, but there appears to be a common language among these forest birds.

While the name Hungry Hollow suggests a poor or poverty stricken place, it is one of the richest places I walk. The creek and the forest provide a cornucopia of floral and faunal sights. The lilies and spring ephemerals are only some of the tangible signs of wealth. They are the first of the spring reincarnates, and the parade of summer plants and animals that follows make up a vivid seasonal wreath. When fall comes, it is a bang of colors, and winter follows in a contrast so evident no one could miss it. I am used to a subtler landscape, having grown up in the southern plain of the Gulf Coast where seasonal changes comes in small packages and almost shyly. But there is nothing subtle or restrained about these woods. They are as bold and vibrant, as audacious and stunning as any place I have ever experienced. And their wealth is incalculable. It is a wealth whose currency is the natural world.

5

One Potato, Two Potato, Three Potato, Four

Over open fields
A farm dwelling here and there
Hay bales cast shadows

OLMSTEAD HILL ROAD becomes Allis Road as it runs along the ridge of Olmstead Hill. With some of the most beautiful vistas of the region, the road overlooks the hills and valleys of Avoca. Fields of potatoes, corn, oats, wheat, kidney beans and soybeans, alfalfa, and clover are as orderly as a checkerboard. The rows of crops, synchronized as a marching band, change every year, but there are always potatoes.

Potatoes have been one of the defining crops for Steuben County throughout its history (Rezelman 2010). "Ever since the days of the Indians, potatoes have been grown in Steuben County" writes Arch Merrill (1954, 158). The county was one of the first large commercial tuber-growing areas in the nation. As early as 1852, the first carload of potatoes was shipped out of Wayland, and as late as 1910, some thirty thousand acres of the county's rugged terrain were planted in potatoes. By 1930 the acreages had dwindled to about seventeen thousand, which is what it is today (Steuben County 1999). The legacy of potatoes

is reflected in such icons as the Boggs potato grader invented in Steuben County and still being made in the village of Atlanta, the Rosch digger, standard equipment on farms at the turn of the century, and the Spalding Rose, an early and popular variety of potato developed in the county. For more than 150 years, potatoes have been king. Even today, with total production of fall potatoes in New York estimated at 5.7 million hundredweight and at 325 hundredweight per acre (*The Courier* 2008), potatoes are still an important crop in the region.

The potatoes grown in these fields, owned by the Stowe family, are primarily chipping potatoes but some are tablestock. Tablestock are those sold whole in the supermarkets, while chipping potatoes are used for making potato chips. Of the thousands of varieties of potatoes, the most common ones are round white, round reds, yellows such as Yukon Gold, and some specialty types like All Blues and fingerlings (Greater Tater 2008). Potatoes are second only to rice in human consumption worldwide. Potato chips are the number one U.S. snack food generating $6 billion each year (Clark 2003). I liked to think that the good earth here in Steuben County provides food that touches the whole country.

The story of how the potato chip came to be, perhaps fittingly, also takes place in New York. One version goes like this: Cornelius Vanderbilt was vacationing in the summer of 1853 in Saratoga Springs at the Moon Lake Lodge. The cook, a Native American named George Crum, prepared fried potatoes, and Vanderbilt (or one of his companions) complained that they were not thin enough. Using a razor blade, Crum grudgingly sliced the potatoes paper thin, fried them, and served them to the complaining guests. To his surprise the potato crunch, or the Saratoga Chip as they were called, caught on and their popularity spread all over the country. Companies like Wise in the 1920s and Lays in the 1930s made fortunes selling potato chips (Harmon 2008).

Some years ago I noticed lots of potatoes spread out and left in the field and thought they might have been left there for the wintering wildlife. When spring came and we were able to walk the road again, the potatoes were gone, so I imagined the deer, turkey, and geese had eaten them. And there are plenty of deer and turkey in the area. In early spring the toms puff up and strut about showing off their vivid scarlet necks and blue heads in the hopes of turning the heads of the dull-colored hens. Adorned in tassels, they fan their tails in displays that might easily compete with the spectacle of a peacock. In summer the flocks move deeper into the woods, and we see them less frequently. But in fall they reappear again to fatten up on the cut grain. Throughout winter, especially on bright sunny days, we see them feeding in the stubble at the edges of the snow-covered cornfields. Their big starburst footprints in the snow make me think of exclamation marks and I imagine them dancing in the moonlight, doing the turkey trot or a wild two-step. One winter I discovered a spot where they must have gathered, because their imprints were everywhere, frozen in the snow like ancient script. The passage might have read, "We're still here and having fun!"

The wild turkey is considered an American conservation success story, because, while their numbers were in the millions in the eighteenth and nineteenth centuries, by the early twentieth century their populations had declined to around thirty thousand (*Bird Conservation* 2008). In New York the wild turkey disappeared in the mid-1840s when the forests were cut for farmland (NYSDEC 2011l). In the 1940s as the woodlands returned, a few turkeys appeared along the New York–Pennsylvania border, and in the 1950s an active restoration program began. Today New York is one of the top ten states with large turkey populations, estimated to be around three hundred thousand. The work of the National Wild Turkey Federation (2010), founded in 1973, was also instrumental in raising the population of wild turkeys from 1.3 million to more than 7 million. I have always found it a paradox that it takes a hunting organization to preserve our wild species, but the truth is that hunting groups have historically been quite effective in wildlife conservation.

For some years we walked this road and were offered the beauty of open fields and patches of woods. In spring, the repetitive *witchedy, witchedy, witchedy* of common yellowthroats echoes across the fields. In late spring, indigo buntings, looking frayed and exhausted from the long journey, arrive and settle in along the woodland edges. They twitter all summer long, joined by red-eyed vireos, whose constant "who am I? vireo! who are you? I don't know!" add a staccato intensity. And when the wood peewees throw in their voices, the woods become a birdsong soundtrack.

Kestrels appear in early spring and by July perch on the electrical wires like notes on sheet music. Bent over in that characteristic hunter's hunch, they look for voles, mice, and lizards. Such illuminations these sparrow hawks present, like glowing lanterns in the sunlight. With two vertical onyx face marks, a rust cape, and blue hood, they are a stunning grassland bird. Smallest of the American falcons, about the size of a robin, they can hover over the field like hummingbirds when hunting. Nesting in woodpecker holes (although some landowners have put up kestrel boxes), they stay well into the fall. When they are on the fly, I think of boomerangs, because their wings are tapered and they slice the sky like a knife.

In August the eastern tailed-blues (*Everes comyntas*) flitter along the road. These dusty, nettle-feeding butterflies have a life cycle that involves a mutalistic relationship with certain species of ants. In the larvae stage, the butterflies, or rather the caterpillars, secrete a sugary liquid, and attendant ants eat this nutritious substance. The ants reciprocate by protecting the caterpillars from predators and parasites, and in some closely related species, the ants actually guide the caterpillars to their proper host plant. The caterpillars produce vibrations called "stridulations," which the ants hear and recognize. The vibrations signal the ants to come and attend. Described lyrically, the butterflies are said to have "children who sing to the ants" (Pierce et al. 2002). I have never heard a caterpillar song, but I imagine its animusic might be a tiny rhythmic composition.

September brings the Milbert's tortoiseshell butterflies as well as the monarchs, who dart and glide about the podded milkweed. Just about the time the purple thistle heads turn to fuzz and winged seeds fill the air with white flakes, the birds begin to move. One afternoon a tree full of migrating redwing blackbirds provided the first signs of winter. Everything begins to take on a certain restlessness in preparation for the coming cold. The white-tailed deer seem more skittish; the red-tailed hawks are more often seen on the hunt; and all the birds, from the field and song sparrows to the blue jays, seem to be in a hurry.

Just off Olmstead Hill Road on Cook Road, Olmstead Cemetery lies in a quiet grove of maples. Like many of the old cemeteries of the county, it is no longer in use, but it is still cared for. Helen Brink (2009) describes these cemeteries as sacred places that hold the history of the region's families and tell the stories of their past. She has traveled more than five thousand miles, located 450 cemeteries, and recorded the names of the dead. Some of the gravestones in this cemetery have a carved hand holding stalks of wheat. This resurrection icon seems particularly fitting for this pastoral place where old maples shade the grounds in summer and cover it in a red quilt in fall. A wrought-iron fence embraces the stones and the gate is always unlocked. There was once a school house on Olmstead Hill, but in 1827 an epidemic of dysentery wiped out all the children (Fox 2002). I don't know if any of them are buried here—many of the gravestones are unreadable—and I once thought it would be a lovely resting place for the innocents. Perhaps the gift of this beautiful spot might offer some compensation for so short a time on earth.

Today the road is shadowed by wind turbines. All along the ridge of Lent Hill the turbines turn. What was once a horizon of spacious skies, an unbroken line where field and sky merged, is now a jagged line of towers and blades. Fields of amber grain and purple hills above a fruited plain are now fenced in metal. Thirty-five turbines and more are expected. In June of 2008 the towers of the turbines went up. Like fists, they rose and proclaimed the sky theirs, the wind theirs, the land theirs. By September the blades were attached. They now dominated the sky. The blades began to turn in 2009.

What has happened here is happening all over the region. The local newspaper, *The Courier*, reports that Turnpike Road in Howard may be the next site of wind turbines (Briggs 2010b). Howard's Town Supervisor states, "We're a small rural town . . . with no way to entice businesses . . . I don't know what else can come to a small rural community." In March 2010, the town board approved the building of twenty-five turbines off Turnpike Road by the company EverPower Renewables (identified as a New York–based firm who will sell the electricity to Steuben Rural Electric Co-op) although in April, construction was reported to be delayed (Briggs 2010a). In return EverPower agreed to a $14 million tax agreement to be paid over twenty years, with $8 million going to the town of Howard. Two of the town trustees who have leased their property with the company said, "EverReady, as far as we know, is a reputable company. They're not going to try and hide anything." With a little Internet searching, I found that EverReady Renewables was purchased in 2009 by Terra Firma Capital Partners, a private equity firm based in the United Kingdom. It owns hundreds of cinemas, hotel chains, motorway service stations, and many more properties all across Europe, and its

CEO, Guy Hands, is the wealthy English financier who moved his residence to avoid paying taxes (Wachman 2009).

Every year my electric bill goes up, my taxes go up, everything goes up, so I understand the pinch of rising costs just as I realize that small rural communities are strapped for funds for schools and municipal services. I also strongly support using cleaner, renewable energy as opposed to burning fossil fuels. But I wonder if we are engaging in a Faustian deal. Is it possible that we might find better ways to live lives of modest material comfort without disturbing the rural character of our land and selling off control of it to distant financial interests that show little responsibility toward our community?

Olmstead Hill Road was one of the first seasonal roads we discovered, and we once walked it regularly. As one of the first, it still has sentimental value, and with its overlooks of hills and valleys, it still commands a lovely view, but the wind turbines make it a different place. It has lost the feel of abundance, and I don't walk the road as much anymore.

6

Seeing the Forests
for the Trees

A loon on the pond
The moonlight painted it there
Soon a memory

THE LOOP WE MOST OFTEN WALK begins with Robie Road, joins
Sonora, then Kettle, and swings back to Robie. It crosses two state
forests, Moss Hill State Forest and Birdseye Hollow State Forest
in Lamoka Valley, a valley speckled with kettle lakes and ponds.
Lamoka and Waneta are the largest lakes, but there are many
smaller ones. In the bends and curves of Mud Creek as it zigzags
through the valley from Mill Pond to the Conhocton River, lies
Sanford, Van Keuren, Round, Peterson, Leonard, and Birdseye
lakes, to name a few.

From lakes and ponds have come some of America's greatest nature writings. It might have started with Thoreau's *Walden*,
but ponds continue to be a significant inspiration for naturalists
and nature writers. John Burroughs (1871) wrote of wildflowers
on ponds near his home in Riverby, New York; Ann Morgan's
*Field Book of Ponds and Streams: An Introduction to the Life of Fresh-
water* (1930) described the ponds of New York, Massachusetts, and
Connecticut; John Kieran (1950) walked ponds in Riverdale, the

Bronx, New York; Joseph Wood Krutch (1969) wrote about living near a small pond in Concord, Massachusetts; and Robert Finch (1983) described the pond of his Cape Cod neighborhood. The list of writers on northeastern ponds and lakes is indeed long. Contemporary writers like Mary Swander write of ponds as places of refuge. She weaves together a visit to Walden, recollections of a childhood pond on her grandmother's farm, and images of her own pond at Fairview School to create a portrait that reflects sanctuary. For her, the pond is a place where she felt whole (Swander 1995, 92–98). Linda Underhill describes a kettle lake—Moss Lake—in nearby Allegany County that is geologically similar to those along these roads. She writes about the pond, part of the Nature Conservancy Preserve purchased in 1957, as off limits to campers and sportsmen, and cites the preserve sign: "This is an inviolate natural area where all living things both plant and animal are to be left undisturbed" (Underhill 1999, 39). Surrounded by a peat bog with floating mats, sphagnum, pitcher plants, sundews, and all the wondrous vegetation of the bog first described by Elizabeth Cook (1973), it is a glorious wetland sanctuary.

Moss Lake has not been managed for human use like the lakes of the Lamoka Valley. Waneta and Lamoka lakes, with their ring of waterfront homes, have been treated with herbicides for years. In an effort to eradicate the invasive, European milfoil (*Myriophyllum spicatum*), New York State Department of Environmental Conservation (NYSDEC) allowed the lakes to be treated with a chlorinated pyridine herbicide called fluordone. The treatment was not effective, so in 2008, a $200,000 grant from NYSDEC was used to treat the lakes again. This time the herbicide, triclopyr, another chlorinated pyridine, was used at one hundred times the original concentration (Perham 2008b, Trondsen 2008). Again in 2009 herbicide treatment continued. Several Steuben County Sierra Club members voiced their concerns, stating that such herbicides are mildly carcinogenic, but they were dismissed as "a few tree-hugger types" by officials of the lake association. When I think of my own choice to use the carcinogen, an artificial sugar, and how I justify it as a means of saving calories, I have to be careful not to be too judgmental regarding those who want an attractive lake free of milfoil. But the fact is that chemicals that kill vegetation, reflected in the suffix -cide, as in biocide, herbicide, pesticide, insecticide, can also kill or damage human cells. We may all be supporters of breast cancer drives and wish to eradicate cancer, but to acknowledge the connection between cancer and the use of certain chemicals, and that there is a price to pay for such chemicals, is a more difficult process.

It is easy to imagine these public forests with their lovely kettle lakes and ponds as refuges or safe places, but that is a myth. One summer I noticed a girl's sneaker beside the road near the pond. Lying on its side, it looked injured with its pink shoelace draped to one side. I was reminded of Lisa Couturier's essay "For All the Girls Who Couldn't Walk into the Woods" (Couturier 2005, 56). She writes "in northeastern forests the biggest threat may be the male *Homo sapiens*." An incident of an assault on a sixteen-year-old girl in these woods suggests that her point is well taken. The girl was riding her bike alone in Birdseye Hollow State Park when she was attacked. Five months later police arrested twenty-eight-year-old Darren McEathron. The report in the *Star-Gazette* (Wilson 2008) claims that McEathron drove by her, hid behind an abandoned vehicle, jumped out, grabbed her, and dragged her into the woods. He had a knife, he threatened her, he struggled with her, and then left for a few minutes. She got up and ran for her life. She escaped (or did she?); McEathron was arrested, tried, and sentenced to eighteen years (Zick 2008).

Other young women have not been so lucky. The murder of twenty-four-year-old Meredith Emerson in Georgia's Voleg State Park and Cheryl Hodges Dunlap in Florida's Apalachicola National Forest by sixty-one-year-old Gary Hilton (Turner 2008) illustrates the danger. Woven into the diary of naturalist Marcia Bonta, as she walks the summer woods of Appalachia, is the rape and murder of a young girl, Melody Curtis (Bonta 1999). Bonta recalls her own narrow escape from a pedophile who tried to entice her into his car when she was in third grade. Bonta writes of the enormous numbers of rapes in this country and ends with a postscript reporting the arrest of Ronald Isenberg, Jr., for the murder of Melody Curtis.

The statistics are obvious, one in three girls is the victim of sexual harassment or rape, but we all know from experience the dangers of some male *Homo sapiens*. And while I feel relatively safe in these woods with my walking partner, our state parks and forests are not safe havens any more than our neighborhoods or our streets or, indeed, our homes.

We tend to think of state forests as environmentally protected lands and they are, but they are not sanctuaries in the truest sense. They are logged, drilled, hunted and trapped on, have roads cut through them for snowmobiles and ATVs, and have electrical transmission lines and gas pipelines running through them. They are, in short, managed for human use and as ways to generate money. NYSDEC states, "All state forests in New York are managed for multiple benefits to serve the needs of the people of New York. Sustained management practices ensure a perpetual supply of timber, a diversity of wildlife habitats, compatible recreational opportunity, and clean water" (NYSDEC 2011f). While there are no housing developments, and aspects of preservation and conservation are used in their management, the state forest is not a nature preserve.

I was reminded of this several years ago when I noticed a section along the road where the black walnuts grew. Loggers had come in and cut the "Demonstration Black Walnut Forest." While I know that the state forests in this region are managed and certified by the National Wildlife Federation's Smart Wood Program, thus, the wood from these forests is "green certified," to my eye, the forest looked diminished and deeply disturbed. The understory was gone and the remaining trees all looked the same. Ecologically, a forest with trees all the same age, size, and species is neither natural nor biologically diverse. The next year some acres near the juncture of Sonora and Kettle Road were clear cut for a timber sale (considered a regeneration cut) and once again I felt like I had lost old friends.

I wonder if NYSDEC's management practices would ever take into account the concept of the forest as a community in its broader sense. I wonder if they might ever give credence to some of the more progressive thinkers such as biologists Bernd Heinrich (1997, 226) and Nalini Nadkarni (2008) who call the forest an ecosystem with many mutual interdependences, or botanist Diana Beresford-Kroeger (2003) who describes trees as promoters of health, or David Suzuki and his colleagues' (2004) testimony to the life-sustaining qualities of trees, or to the Buddhist environmentalist Stephanie Kaza (1993) who advocates a spiritual engagement with trees. There are some who believe that forests should not be managed at all (Rogel 2003). While NYSDEC has made progress with efforts at sustainability, their mission is anthropocentric, and their concept of a healthy forest is a managed forest. Clearly, the foresters of NYSDEC try to manage forests in what they believe to be the best ways, but when I see a clear cut or even a selective cut, I feel as though I had been cut. And yet for all the cutting of trees, I am grateful for these forests, even if they are managed like a cornfield and treated as a commodity.

The history of New York's state forests begins around the turn of the century (NYSDEC 2011d). In 1890 New York was predominately farmland with only 20 percent forest, but today forest makes up 62 percent. Nearly 20 percent of that belongs to the state and is state land. The beginnings of the state forests program are rooted in the Great Depression of the late 1920s and the mass exodus of people from the worn-out, hardscrabble farms of New York to the Midwest. These events resulted in abandoned lands. In 1928 the State Reforestation Commission was formed, and a year later the State Reforestation Law was passed "to retire farmlands from agricultural use." The Hewitt Amendment of 1931 authorized the Conservation Department to acquire land for reforestation, and by 1933, the Civilian Conservation Corps (the CCC) had thousands of young men planting trees on the state land. Legislation such as the Park and Recreation Land Acquisition Act of 1960 and the Environmental Quality Bond Act of 1972 and 1986 expanded land acquisition. Today there are seven hundred thousand acres of state forests, and in Steuben County 2.6 percent of the county is state forest.

The two state forests we walk, Moss Hill and Birdseye Hollow, were acquired from power companies: Moss Hill from the Lamoka Power Company that originally planned a hydroelectric project but sold the land when funds dried up during the Depression (NYSDEC 2011d) and Birdseye Hollow from Keuka Lake Power Company (NYSDEC 2011a). Moss Hill was farmed for about 130 years, from the 1790s to the 1910s. Abandoned in 1910–1929, the state acquired the 1,815 acres in the 1930s. Several natural gas wells were drilled after World War II, abandoned in the 1950s, and drilled again in the 1990s. One early well, called the "bubbler," remained open and vented gas for fifty years. Several fires in the area were the result of that well. But, of course, now energy companies like Fortuna Energy Company have recognized the value of such gas, have leased the land from the state, and are busy tapping it for profits.

Two forest types typically characterize the Allegheny Plateau, the oak-hickory and the beech-maple forest with white pine and hemlock as components. The forests here are a mixture of these forest types. They are also considered secondary forests which means they have grown up on land that was once farmed, in contrast to primary forests, which are forests on land not farmed. Primary forests were, of course, once logged and cut but they retain some of the qualities of the old original forests. There are sections of primary forest on some state forests, but they are usually in areas more difficult to access. There are no true old-growth forests in Steuben County.

Where Mud Creek crosses Robie is warblerville. Yellow warblers, chestnut-sided, blackburnian, and yellow rumps are common, but there are also black and white, pine, black-throated green, and black-throated blues as well. The wood warblers seem to like this lazy creek. Flycatchers flit through the trees; a belted kingfisher is often heard rattling about; and the meowing of catbirds and the nasal nays of nuthatches offer a smorgasbord of birdsong. The barely audible, high-pitched trills of cedar waxwings make me think of dog whistles. Mixed with the croaking of green frogs "slack strings plucked by heavy thumbs" (Bishop 1995, 56), it is a jazzy zone.

In late summer cardinal flowers sprout from the banks and against the lush green; they are jolting in their crimson flashes. The cardinal flower was a favorite among the American floral women of the nineteenth century. Almira Phelps in "Familiar Lectures on Botany" writes, "Do not be deceived by the prettiness of flowers. Beneath their delightful surfaces lie profound lessons about the design of the natural world" (Phelps 1829). I think she might have found some important truths about what attracts humans in the red petals of these attention-getting flowers.

Joe Paddock tells a story of a local boat builder from Bradford who used Mill Pond for his boat-building business. His answer to product transport was to dam Mud Creek. When the boats were completed and ready to be moved, he blew up the dam and let the massive wave of water carry them to the Conhocton River. Sometimes after a hard rain when the creek level is high, I imagine a flotilla of newly constructed boats riding the wave down to the river.

In the summer woods we see an occasional scarlet tanager, Baltimore orioles, red-breasted grosbeaks, and red-eyed vireos. Blue jays and red-tailed hawks are here all year round. Sapsucker, red-bellied, downy, and hairy woodpeckers are the small wood-carvers; the master carvers are the pileated woodpeckers. A resident pair lives in the woods, and we spot them or hear them nearly every time we walk. Their calls are loudest in summer, but even in fall, their drumming echoes throughout the woods. Hop-scotching from one tree to another, they travel the woods intent on recording their clan in the old trees. They carve long rectangular holes in the ancient trunks and keep working them until the trees resemble totem poles. All along the road, their carved drumming trees are monuments to their presence.

In April coltsfoot sprout from the barren ground, bend, flower, and color the roadside yellow. Then trout lilies carpet the forest floor with their mottled binary leaves and sprinkle the ground with yellow stars. A smattering of trillium bloom in the low areas, but the road runs mostly on the slope, so they are not especially abundant. Patches of periwinkles and lily of the valley grow near the juncture of Mud Creek and Sonora, and wild geraniums add a touch of violet. Near Sanford Pond, skunk cabbages uncoil like alien purple pods and become sculptures of pure chlorophyll. Mary Oliver writes of these odd plants, "turnip-hearted . . . green caves . . . what blazes the trail is not necessarily pretty" (Oliver 2004, 11).

Later in the spring the ferns begin to embellish the road-side, and I think of ladies' hats from my childhood. The sensitive ferns that die off so quickly at first frost remind me of my grand-mother's wide-brimmed gardener's hat; the bracken ferns make me think of Methodist churchgoers whose lacy veils were ever so modest; and the fragrant wood ferns make me think of those brimmed homemakers who wore Evening in Paris perfume given to them on their birthdays by their children.

As summer rolls forth, the broadleaf trees grow lush and the road becomes a tunnel of green. Most of the trees in these woods are young, densely packed, and produce lots of shade. So out of necessity, the shorter plants have to be shade tolerant. Blackberry brambles swing their white flowery vines in graceful arches, and by mid-September the roadside is full of bluestem goldenrod (*Solidago caesia*). Of the hundred species of goldenrods, this native species is a forest goldenrod, more shade tolerant and delicate than the aggressive "take over the meadow" one.

The butterflies of the road appear like idle thoughts, small flashes of color and motion, then gone. In spring, the spring azures, the red admirals, the cabbage whites, and the snouts prevail. Summer brings the mourning cloaks and eastern swallowtails, and in September, sulfur and Milbert's tortoiseshell butterflies fleck the roadside. The slugs come out on warm fall days and leave slime trails that sparkle in the sunlight like strips of cellophane. Then in winter when all the butterflies have disappeared, the chocolate puddles plated with ice become a source of crunch. We step on them, listen to them crack and make wishes for the butterflies' return.

A few cellar holes mark the old homesteads that once dotted the land, and one summer day, we stepped off the road to explore one. The remains of recalcitrant things—pieces of metal, rusted and bent, and old glass—lay among the loose stones of the crumbling foundation. One cobalt bottle peeked out from the rubble, and I couldn't resist picking it up, but when lifted, it was broken. There was an old Vicks salve bottle, a dark brown medicine bottle that may have held iodine, and a few clear glass ones with smooth tops indicating they might have been stoppered with cork. They were all cracked, chipped, or broken, not a whole one in the bunch.

Posted signs at the northeast end of Robie where it joins Sonora mark the land belonging to the Zyla family. Indigo buntings perch in the willows just beyond the old cellar hole. It is a perfect habitat for them because of the tiny streamlet that trickles most of the summer from the forest through the meadow to Mud Creek. An old cemetery along Sonora has a pond behind it, and common yellowthroats sing in the brambles that border the road. Farther south, an old barn and an abandoned house once stood beneath a groove of old oaks. Several summers ago a couple of boys burned the house down (Zick 2006). From the report, it appeared as if the arson was committed out of boredom. The house belonging to the Zyla family was full of family heirlooms, and the family grieved the loss of those memories. I miss that old house as well and wonder at the disrespect that seems to fill the minds and actions of some young people.

The forests accessed by these roads have seen much of the affairs of humans: attacks on young girls, vandalism, logging, drilling, so many impacts. How could the forest not view us humans as anything other than a violent species, concerned with only our own self-interests? But for all the acts of destruction, for all the dangers that exist here, as they do in the world in general, I cannot help but love these woods. And while I hope the dangers never touch me as I walk them, I do so with gratitude that we have these state forest lands.

7

Back to the Land

In the winter tree
A long-eared owl silhouette
Gained by being seen

LATE ONE AFTERNOON on Harrisburg Hollow Road, I encountered a barred owl. I first saw it on the wing as it flew down the road and into the dark woods. Walking toward where it entered the woods, I spotted it far back in the dark branches perched on a pine limb. We stared at one another for a while, and then it turned and flew away. I can recall every encounter I have ever had with owls, and every time, I feel it is a small miracle. I believe that the encounters are a message. I don't mean the sort of messages Hedwig, Pigwidgeon, and the other mail-carrying owls of Harry Potter convey or the messages Native Americans believe owls send. I mean the kinds of communications that are not about details. The message I get from owls is their presence. It is like thinking of someone you love and suddenly that person is there, and it is wonderful just to be in his or her presence.

We sometimes begin where the road makes a sharp right and becomes a narrow dirt road. The woods to the south belong to the Ferris family. Other times we begin farther up where it makes a sharp left and borders a long pasture. The posted signs read, "Poole Farms, Wheeler, NY." On the fence posts, bluebirds perch poised

with the confidence of ace pilots, and on the other side, a pond harbors yellow-rump warblers. A line of red pines forms a windbreak where field and song sparrows flitter among the branches almost all year long. The spot is known as Puckerbush, according to Doug Bigelow and Martha Ferris Bigelow. The name comes from the youthful parking and smooching that once took place here. The only puckering done now is by the phoebes and juncos, who like the brambles in the small dip of the road where a streamlet crosses.

The road passes through open fields and woods, so the wildflowers are both meadow and woodland species. In the open sections, the wildflowers paint a border of vivid colors and rich textures throughout the spring, summer, and fall. There are day lilies, bluebells, vervain, Queen Anne's lace, chicory, cow vetch, phlox, milkweed, and burdock. Nowhere else do we see vervain (*Verbena hastata*) so abundant and healthy. Their fancy spikes in August decorate the roadside with blue candelabras until late in September. The woodland flowers begin with trout lilies and trillium, move to mayapples and woodland sunflowers, and taper off with goldenrods. Interruption, cinnamon, and sensitive fern add green arabesques to the sparsely inhabited shade.

One fall a flock of pheasants dressed in their finest gathered in the road and scattered like the breaking of the rack in billiards when we approached. Occasionally, we see raccoon, white-tailed deer, and the solitary skunk ambling across the road. One warm sunny summer afternoon I spotted a dead skunk in the road. The lyrics of a funky tune popular in the early 1970s, "Dead Skunk in the Middle of the Road" by Loudon Wainwright II immediately popped into my mind. I don't know why this song rises up from the gray matter of my memory whenever I see a dead skunk in the road. Maybe it has something to do with the song's catchy beat, its zydeco rhythm, and blood-and-guts images. It is such a silly tune, and I never know whether to chuckle or admonish myself when the lyrics roll through my thoughts.

Sniffing to make sure the scent was tolerable, I eased over to the roadkill and leaned down to get a closer look. It was a young striped skunk, and I was about to make a remark to my walking partner, when the skunk moved. It opened one eye, stretched a leg, and twitched its tail. My mind went into flight mode and with the agility of a tai chi master, I backed away as quickly and as slowly as I could. The skunk rose up from its sleep, shook itself out, and waddled off. I was relieved we parted on such good terms, neither one of us the worse for the encounter.

While skunks seem to inspire a certain comic element, from the caricature, Pepe Le Pew, to phrases like "He's as welcome as a skunk at a lawn party" or "Never kick a skunk," only a few naturalists show much interest in them, and not many poets have used them metaphorically. Dallas Lore Sharp, watching a family of young skunks rolling and frolicking in the leaves, describes them as "humpty-dumpty babies" (Sharp 1901, 285). Marcia Bonta (1991, 14) describes their courting and mating behavior as "a rough affair," and their defensive behavior as a last resort when "it stamps its front feet as warning, then rudely turns its back, lifts its tail, and finally shoots." The spray contains some of the nastiest-smelling chemicals around, volatile sulfur-containing compounds, and is used not only against threats from other animals, but female skunks are reported to spray unwanted males looking to mate. In a poem entitled, "Skunk Hour," Robert Lowell writes for (and perhaps about) Elizabeth Bishop, she "drops her ostrich tail, / and will not scare" (Lowell 1959). Perhaps that undaunted quality of immovability expressed in Lowell's poem is a function of one of the most extraordinary and effective nonviolent defense mechanisms in the animal kingdom.

The road borders PeaceWeavers land; their retreat is called Thunder Mountain. The PeaceWeavers are what I think of as back-to-the-land folks (PeaceWeavers 2008). They began nearly twenty years ago as "a group of people who wanted to activate greater peace in their lives and in the world." Over the years, they have evolved into a community that offers peace gatherings, retreats, and workshops on sustainable living. They give programs on healing and spiritual awareness and grow organic vegetables and grains (Murray 2009). The PeaceWeavers sell their produce to Wegmans, a family-run grocery-store chain known for its policies supporting locally grown food, or donate it to local food pantries. In 2008 the sixty families of the PeaceWeavers grew and donated hundreds of pounds of food to Turning Point and the Pro-Action Senior Nutrition Program (*The Courier* 2009). Known for their local community action, the PeaceWeavers award scholarships to local high school students, are active in environmental issues, and participate in local politics. Their retreat has also served as a refuge for displaced people such as those affected by Hurricane Katrina.

One evening I attended a program at their retreat and before the speaker began, the Weavers' drum circle played for us. The drums beat out a collective rhythm, rising and falling in intensity, changing in rapidity, altering the pattern again and again, and finally resolving into a calm silence. I felt grateful that there are people in this world who are willing to examine the way they live, who have decided to put aside some of the modern conveniences and complexities that result in heavy environmental costs, and are trying to live simply and close to the earth in a compassionate way, with an environmental ethic of care.

The back-to-the-land movement in its purest form probably refers to those who live off the land deriving income exclusively from it in a sustainable way. The writings of Ralph Borsodi (Loomis 1992, 2008) in the 1920s, 1930s, and 1940s perhaps represent one of the earliest voices in that movement. Author of numerous books and articles, he was a true homesteader, not only living on the land in what became known as the decentralist movement but also establishing a school and organizing small experimental communities. The writings of Helen and Scott Nearing (1954) in their classic *Living the Good Life: How to Live Sanely and Simply in a Troubled World* might be the first postmodern example of back-to-the-land accounts. In the 1960s and 1970s, Stewart Brand's *The Whole Earth Catalog* came into being, and that collection embodied the ideas reflected in the beginnings of the American environmental movement (Kirk 2007). Since the 1980s there have been hundreds, perhaps thousands, of books and writings that offer accounts and advice on how to live on the land.

While we might imagine the "back-to-the-land movement" as referring to those who derive their living from the land, with the exception of the Amish, there are actually few who truly do so, although today many are trying. Most accounts of country life or rural life were and are still being written by those whose incomes come from other sources. The "country life movement," which began in the nineteenth century with the fundamental restructuring of American society due to industrialization (Bowers 1974), peaked around 1900 to 1920. Writers who described the rural life gained popularity when increasing numbers of people yearned to get back to nature. Writers like columnist Hal Borland (Borland 1957), who wrote for *The New York Times* in the 1940s, 1950s, 1960s, and 1970s, and Verlyn Klinkenborg (Klinkenborg 2003), who currently writes *The New York Times* column "Rural Life," continued to reflect the beauty and joy of the rural setting, but they are like most folks: they might live in the country, but they do not really live off the land in a sustainable way. Some critics have claimed that some of these writers promoted an agrarian myth or, at best, reflected a contradiction (Bowers 1974).

The well-known contemporary nature writer Kathleen Dean Moore, writing in an essay entitled, "Landing," (Moore 2003) captures what I think is the modern meaning of back to the land: "*Land* is a noun, a solid, a place you come home to. *Land* is a set of relationships—ecosystems, hydrological cycles, ocean currents, neighborhoods, and nitrogen cycles, and the energy that flows among them. But *land* is also a verb, an action that people take: To land is to come into contact again (finally, blessedly) with the actual earth, a place that welcomes you, nourishes you, protects you, lifts you with relief." She continues by explaining how she has met many people who are engaged in the work of landing, coming back to their places, people who have made the decision to live in a way that does not harm the natural systems of the earth. This may not mean living off the land entirely or deriving income from it exclusively, but it does mean having intimate and caring relationships with the land and the people who call it home.

Just over the hill west of Harrisburg Hollow, a community of Amish nestled in the folds of Wheeler calls these vales home. They grow vegetables, run dairies, make lumber, raise chickens, and live off the land of those wooded hills. Their houses are simple, their clothes are unadorned, they drive black-box buggies, and every time I encounter them, I am transported back in time to an earlier century. The colors of the Amish are winter: "purple, gray, black, blue, and white . . . black buggies, black hats, black lunch pails" writes Cathleen Miller (2002, 139), and yet they often have been the source of refuge. Mary Swander writes about living among the Amish to regain her health (Swander 1995); and in much of our fiction the Amish serve as refuge. The idea of their communities as sanctuary seems almost a given (Harper 1996, Picoult 2000, Lewis and Lewis, 2001).

Beginning in May, the Amish bring their produce to the local farmers' market, and one summer I wrote a poem that begins in that setting. The Amish, and especially David Kline (1990), have always inspired me to praise the good harvest that comes from the earth and to believe in the beauty of simple things.

Music for a Mild Day *(in answer to Mary Oliver's*
"Who Ever Made Music of a Mild Day?")

Yesterday morning the farmers' market was an orchestral
    harvest,
summer squash the size of oboes, toe-tapping tomatoes, brassy
    melons,

beets in percussion fists dense as the heads of kettle drumsticks,
wax beans thin as piccolos, butternuts plump as violas.

From a barefoot Amish girl and her mother I bought a basket of
    sweet cherries
and all day long I popped them in my mouth like candy. At
    every taste

I felt I should sing a hymn of praise to all the red and yellow
    things of summer.
Later in the evening the full moon came up over the hills, the
    color of those cherries

And I heard the coyotes yipping until moonlight covered the
    world in silver.
Every creature must have its own song of praise for the seasons

And music can be made for every day,
mild or wild or otherwise.

While the Amish and their lifestyle have a certain appeal, it is
a way of living different from my own. Their religious faith and
rigid roles for women are doctrines I could never accept, and their
lack of conveniences, I would find discomforting, but their sim-
plicity, honesty, and intimacy with the natural world are qualities I admire. In many ways the Amish and the PeaceWeavers are
alike, and I have the utmost respect and admiration for those who
can live simply, close to the natural world, and with the purpose
of living honorably.

Living near the Amish community is the poet, Michael Czarnecki, and his family. Michael, who is a seasonal roads walker, operates the small family-run press called FootHills Publishing, and for twenty-five years, he has published the works of our local poets and writers. It seems fitting that our poets, the PeaceWeavers, and the Amish would share a tangential place.

When we first started walking Harrisburg Hollow Road, the road was a joy to experience, but during the past several years, I have felt a growing sense of uneasiness. Two years ago, a burned-out abandoned car was left in the middle of the road. Reports in the newspaper of arrests for assault and vandalism gave the men's addresses as Harrisburg Hollow Road. One evening, several boys in a big blue pickup came speeding up the road spattering mud on us as they dug deep trenches in the wet surface. They added to the growing piles of trash by pitching out beer cans and Styrofoam fast food boxes as they sped along. Perhaps these events explain my uneasiness. Even with the nearby PeaceWeavers and the Amish just over the hill, I have been unable to regain the feeling of comfort on the road. I find I don't walk the road as much anymore. And I have never seen the owl again.

8

There Was a Crooked Lake

Urbana Road

On sloping hillsides
Row upon row the vineyards
Flowing with the land

THEY DROVE UP in their shiny new Lexus, knocked on my door, and introduced themselves as the Joneses (not their real names). They had come to my home to ask for easement rights. My partner and I had declined an earlier written request from their lawyer— we wanted to keep impacts to the land as minimal as possible— but Mr. and Mrs. Jones were now on my doorstep asking to discuss the matter. They were nice, pleasant people, and he explained that he wanted to run a phone line from a nearby Empire station (the rural phone company) across our land to his property so that he could have a connection to his new house. They had cell phones, he said, but he wanted a land line for his security system, a very expensive one, he added. They had a waterfront home near Rochester, and they were now building this "vacation house in the woods" overlooking Keuka Lake. To pay for the house, he was dividing the property, selling off a strip of six acres that bordered our land, and asking $10,000 per acre.

Urbana Hill was once covered with vineyards, much of them belonging to Gold Seal Wineries, a vineyard dating back to the 1860s. We had purchased ten acres of the old vineyards in the

1990s, and since that time had been trying to restore it to native grasses and trees. We planted a native cultivar of switchgrass and a hundred red oaks, white oaks, and black walnuts. In 1998, a nearby landowner bought the land south of us and logged it. The loggers went onto our land, cut some of our trees and left the site a mess. While timber theft is common all over the country (Saulny 2008), it is especially troublesome in rural New York (NYSDEC 2011j). Since there was no proof of who actually cut the trees on our land or who was responsible, there was little we could do. Legal action can take years and requires considerable expense.

After logging, that same landowner divided up the land and sold it off in smaller lots. It changed hands several more times, and one of the parcels now belonged to the Joneses, who had built their "vacation house" on it. The Joneses also wanted to break up the land again, selling part of it to pay for their new house. Around Keuka Lake, land fragmentation is happening at an increasingly alarming rate. With lake views in demand, dozens of McMansions have gone up along Middle Road as well as development around the entire seventy-mile shoreline of Keuka Lake. The old vineyards, the farm fields, and the woods are being carved up and turned into housing developments, and country homes for the wealthy are expanding beyond the lakeshore into the hills.

In January 2008, we discovered loggers on our land again. This time they had been hired by another neighbor. Loggers cut 108 trees from her eight acres, hauled off about half of them, and left the others lying on the roadside—they were not worth the money to haul them to the mill. She claimed she didn't really want to cut the trees but owed back taxes and had to get the money to save her home. We hired a survey team to reflag the lines, but the loggers still managed to cut some of our trees, and they ran over all the young oak trees we had planted along the border.

One spring morning out in the field checking trees, I heard the cry of the pileated woodpecker that once nested in the old shagbark hickory along the road. The loggers had cut her nesting tree. The old tree, full of holes, was deemed worthless and left on the roadside to rot. Her call seemed the most sorrowful cry, and I was struck by an overwhelming sense of grief and futility. Our attempts to care for the land, to keep it in a natural state seemed "a candle in the wind." Not only have we been unable to protect our land from logging, but all around us the land was being fragmented and turned into housing developments. Even though we have been trying to treat the land in a respectful way, trying to support wildlife, leaving it as natural as possible, those around us were not. Our efforts seemed fruitless in this ever-growing black hole of desire our citizens seem to be sinking into.

Urbana Road runs uphill from the old Gold Seal Winery on Keuka Lake and joins Middle Road, which parallels the lake. Middle Road dips up and down, crosses a gully, curves through woods, and opens up onto what were once hay fields and vineyards. Much of the land has become lawns surrounding huge houses, and there is a stable where show horses summer. But vineyards still occupy some of the land. At the end of Middle Road is Dr. Konstantin Frank's Vinifera Wine Cellars, a family-owned vineyard since 1930. Well known for some of the finest wines in the country (Alexander 2007), it is one of a hundred or more wineries in the region (Klees 2008). Sometimes, especially in winter, the sweet smell of fermentation from the winery drifts in on the breeze as we walk past the carefully pruned hedges of grapevines.

While some of the local vineyards are family owned, others are corporate owned. The great names in wine, Taylor, Great Western, and Gold Seal, were bought and resold by corporate conglomerates over the years. Nearby Bully Hill Winery, for example, was acquired by Coca Cola in the 1970s, sold to Seagram, Inc. in the 1980s, and is now owned by Constellation Brands, Inc., the largest wine company in the world (Feulner 2007). The two closest vineyards, Heron Hill Winery established in the 1970s and Keuka Lake Winery only a few years old, are family owned. Heron Hill is owned by John and Josephine Ingles of Naples, New York, and Keuka Lake Winery, by Mel and Dorothee Goldman (Klees 2008). The Ingles employ sound, sustainable ecological practices and biodynamic farming in their vineyards using little pesticides and hiring local pickers. An article in the *Star-Gazette* describes Mr. Goldman as a former Peace Corps volunteer, the developer of a consulting firm called New Era, and a member of the World Bank, who worked on economic, agriculture, and rural development issues (Richards 2007).

The view from Middle Road is spectacular. The lake and sky mirror one another and the hillsides are a collage of forest, fields, and vineyards. The texture of the land reflects the season, shades of green in spring and summer, an autumnal mosaic in fall, and brown, gray, and white in winter. Even though I love the landscape's immediate beauty, I know this particular portrait is a recent one. The slopes of Keuka Lake in the 1800s were almost completely covered in vineyards (House and Mitchell 2008). Steamboats buzzed up and down the lake carrying passengers and cargo; the lake was a busy place in those days.

Before the first European settlers, the land was forest. Long before that, in geological time, the land underwent a series of enormous transitions. According to our local geology expert, Peter Robbins, 350 million years ago it was a tropical sea, and rivers flowed into it carrying loads of sediments. The sediments were deposited layer upon layer and compressed into rock. The land uplifted forming a great plateau, and rivers cut through it emptying into lakes. About two million years ago, the ice came, and periods of cold and warm resculpted the land. Thick sheets of ice a mile or more deep moved across the plateau scouring it, deepening the rivers, and depositing debris at the moraines. The glaciers moved forward and retreated, forward and retreated, again and again. The last one, about ten thousand years ago, left valleys of varying depths with hilltops all about the same height. The hilltops around here are not mountain peaks but rather the remnants of the ancient plateau known as the peneplain.

We think of the ice age as a long-gone event, but according to Linda Underhill (1999), "we still live in an ice age" (119) and "listen to the songs of the ice" (123). When winter grasps its icy fingers around the lake, I think she may be right. While some of the lake freezes in winter—it is 183 feet deep—ice forms only in the shallower northern end most years; although in 1925, the entire lake froze, and folks went ice fishing from Penn Yan to Hammondsport. The waters of the lake are relatively clean and unpolluted (Halfman and O'Neill 2009) due, in part, to the active protection and progressive actions of the Keuka Lake Association. Established in 1954, the organization conducts water-monitoring programs and controls the wastewater/watershed (Keuka Lake Association 2008). The lake's watershed is large, more than 110,000 acres. We have counted 135 streams and streamlets on the east side of the lake alone—it is about twenty miles from Hammondsport to Penn Yan, and if extrapolated to include the whole lake, there could be hundreds of streams feeding the lake.

We used to see an abundance of wildlife on our walks. One year we caught a family of red foxes playing like puppies in the wooded gully. In the shafts of sunlight, their fur gleamed like lit matches. We once saw ruffed grouse, the bird known as America's little peacock (Scott 1980, 139), explode across the road, race through the fields, and disappear. Red and gray squirrels, rabbits, chipmunks, and white-tailed deer were plentiful. We rarely see them anymore.

We still see birds. In early summer, the red-winged blackbirds descend on the fields in droves and claim the meadows, taking "up a musically raucous serenade, a talking in tongues" (Carroll 2004, 54). Bobolinks and meadowlarks still nest in the few remaining hay fields, but their numbers are declining every year. Baltimore orioles, cedar waxwings, bluebirds, and common yellowthroats inhabit the thickets along the road. Mockingbirds have appeared in recent years and these birds, which Harper Lee warns us never to kill, seem to be surviving. Barn and tree swallows seine the sky above the fields for insects, and sparrows are a constant twitter.

The plants along the road are always interesting. One summer in late August we discovered a patch of peppermint (*Mentha x piperita*) in bloom. Because it spreads and takes over an area so quickly, it is considered an invasive species. The plant is a sterile hybrid of water mint (*M. aquatica*) and spearmint (*M. spicata*) and represents one of the world's oldest medicines. Archeological records dating back ten thousand years claim peppermint was used for a variety of medicinal purposes. I think finding it is a good sign, much like finding a four-leaf clover. Other plants in the mint family, such as hairy wood mint (*Blephilia hirsuta*) and bugleweed (*Ajuga reptans*), come and go. The fields and ditches are also full of wildflowers: Queen Anne's lace, chicory, and orange day lilies in July. Common milkweed and goldenrod appear later on.

The land around Keuka Lake, as with all the Finger Lakes, has always been one in flux, a landscape of change. Once it was an ancient sea, once a massive ice sheet, once forests, farmland, once vineyards, but I wonder about the most recent changes. The land is being broken up and splintered, a process that causes habitat and wildlife loss. Such fragmentation so that the rich can enjoy McMansions and lake views may not be the most respectful way to treat our land. We humans, in our insatiable appetite for luxury and status, never seem to question this "acceptable lust" (Lewis 2009, 76) or what our extravagance costs. And if we do ask that question, the answer seems to be that our fellow species don't matter much in our quest for a comfort that may, in truth, be opulence. I understand the desire to have a waterfront home. Who would not want a home on this beautiful lake and if I won the lotto, I would be sorely tempted to buy a house on the lake, but can we afford to continue to splinter it and to deplete it until there is nothing left but a minimalist humanscape, "a landscape being stripped of it original meaning" (Carroll 2009, 5)? And what does this loss do to "the less easily observed ecology of the psyche?" (Arthur 2009, 6) Does the loss of meadowlarks diminish our imagination? Are our moments less rich when we replace bobolinks with lawns where lavish mansions sit? What happens to our psyche when we cause a species to go extinct? Are we denying both our biological past and its future? If extinction is the shutting of an evolutionary door so nothing more will ever come from it, that path forward is closed. Meadowlarks have been singing for millions of years, longer than humans have existed; they are part of what was and I hope what will be. Yet we seem unaware that we are impoverishing not only the present, but the past and the future as well.

9

A Road for All Reasons

Mackey Road

Where ancestors lie
Wild columbine grace the stones
Heads nod and bow low

THE ROAD CLIMBS UPHILL from the Conhocton River near Avoca, bends through woods, and runs along a small stream. Just beyond the final upward curve, a natural gas facility sits nestled in the hillside. Beyond that posted signs indicate the woods belong to a private hunting club, and where Reservoir Road joins Mackey, the forest has been cut for timber. Corn and soybean fields come next. Farther along the road, the Avoca New York State Electric and Gas (NYSEG) substation looks out onto the wind turbines of the distant Cohocton Ridge. The road then cuts through hay fields and a small stand of hardwoods, curves downhill past an old cemetery, and finally dips down to Smith Pond.

We generally begin Mackey at the hilltop near the Avoca Natural Gas storage site. The facility consists of a pumping station and some underground salt caverns built in the mid-1990s. The facility once seemed unobtrusive, but now the sight of any natural gas pipes reminds me of the contentious issues of new gas drilling in the region. The storage caverns have been bought and sold numerous times; currently they are owned by El Paso Inc., a multinational corporation and largest natural gas pipeline company in North America (El Paso 2008). The chairman, president and CEO of El Paso, Douglas L. Foshee, was executive vice president and CEO of Halliburton from 2001–3 and is a trustee of AIG's Credit Facility Trust and chair of the Houston branch of the Federal Reserve Bank of Dallas (AIG was one of the companies implicated in the recent financial collapse and federal bailouts costing taxpayers billions; Spitzer et al. 2009). El Paso purchases natural gas from Fortuna Energy, Inc., another multinational and a subsidiary of Talisman Energy, formerly British Petroleum, or BP–Canada, a company that also has a complex history of mergers and acquisitions. Fortuna Energy has traditional natural gas wells all over the county. So one multinational company is drilling the natural gas, and another is distributing and selling it to the small town of Avoca—the very place from which the gas originates.

Fortuna Energy, Inc., is also one of several gas production companies that are major players in the recent controversy arising from the discovery of large natural gas deposits in the area. For decades, gas has been extracted from the Trenton Black River formation and other deposits, and there are wells all over the north and northeast part of the county. Natural gas extraction from these wells has not been extensively damaging to the environment because the gas is comparatively easy to extract.

The discovery of the Marcellus Shale formation is a different matter. What makes this deposit problematic is that, while it may be the third largest natural gas deposit in the world with the potential for huge profits, the gas is difficult to extract because it is dispersed throughout the porous rock (shale) of the formation (Krauss 2008). In other parts of the United States, this kind of natural gas has been extracted by a process called hydraulic fracturing or hydrofracking. Developed by oil-extraction companies (Halliburton is listed as a pioneer of the technique), it has resulted in extensive environmental damages (Andhara and Sitkin 2008). Large amounts of water (as much as one to five million gallons for each well) with toxic solvents, lubricants, and other chemicals are forced under extreme pressure down into the shale to squeeze out the gas. The possibility for contaminating the aquifers and the region's water sources is clearly an issue (Earthworks 2006, Kingsley 2008, Sumi 2008).

Although hearings by NYSDEC (2011e) were conducted throughout 2008, 2009, 2010, and 2011 in which many voices raised concerns about the environmental impact of such drilling, NYSDEC seems likely to approve drilling permits. NYSDEC's commissioner states that hydrofracking will take place many thousands of feet underground, well below any groundwater zone (typically only hundreds of feet below the surface) and, thus, presents no problem. Perhaps this signals a compliance with the drilling industry (NYSDEC 2011c). With the passage of the Energy Policy Act of 2005 (U.S. Committee on Energy and Commerce 2007) providing exemptions for the oil and gas industry from the Safe Drinking Water Act and the Clean Water Act, and with the NYSDEC admission that the agency is not prepared for the level of regulatory enforcement needed for drilling operations in the Marcellus Shale (Wilber 2009), there is likely to be little adequate state or federal protection regarding these extraction activities. What will happen to the region's water and air, not to mention the communities' infrastructure and landscape, may prove to be the most disastrous environmental event ever to occur to this region (Shaleshock 2009). Landowners, eager for lease money from the gas companies, seem oblivious to the problems of hydrofracking and have not responded with any sense of alarm at this potential pollution. Groups such as Citizens for Healthy Communities, the Finger Lakes Group of the Sierra Club, and others have tried to get information to the public, but the promise of lease money, jobs and a boom economy seems to be blinding the citizenry.

Beyond the storage caverns, posted hunting land is marked by signs that read "4/10 Club, P.O. Box, Minetto, New York." Sections along this part of the road have been logged several times, once in 2007 and again in 2008. The landing sites where the cut trees were dragged for transporting were restored, and there are no deep ruts or waste wood left over. The lumbering site was kept small and by 2011 there was little visible sign of disturbance.

A little farther south, an electrical transformer station sits like a metallic shrine to electric power. The sign that has been there for years reads "New York State Electric and Gas Corporation (NYSEG)." The name might imply a public utilities company owned or managed by the state. But it is not a public utility. NYSEG and Rochester Gas and Electric were purchased by a private company, Energy East, Corp., who then sold it to the Spain-based multinational corporation Iberdrola for $4.6 billion (Richtmyer 2008). Iberdrola is identified by Wikipedia as "the world's largest private electric utilities company, [and] operations include generation, transmission, distribution, and marketing of electricity and natural gas." The multinational company currently provides about 16 percent of all the electricity to the state of New York, owns 50 percent of the Maple Ridge Wind Farm in Lewis County (the state's largest wind farm), and intends to invest $2 billion in wind power projects in New York (Gallagher 2008a).

During the summer and fall of 2008, articles in the local papers reported the events that led up to Iberdrola's owning NYSEG. New York state's Public Service Commission (PSC), the commission that sets rates and provides oversight of the state's utilities, held hearings and discussions regarding this purchase. PSC, whose role is to protect consumers from unreliable service and unfair rate hikes, raised the issue of whether the multinational should be able to both generate and distribute gas (Stinson 2008). During the PSC hearings some rather odd events occurred. For example, one commissioner, Cheryl Buley, who initially raised concerns about the buyout and questioned whether state subsidies for wind power for Iberdrola would be too expensive for the state (Gallagher 2008b), resigned (*The Leader* 2008). Another commissioner left as well.

After months of hearings by the PSC, political pressure was exerted, and the sale was approved. The support of Senator Charles Schumer and virtually every major political figure in the state, for the purchase of NYSEG by Iberdrola ensured that the buyout was a done deal (Gallagher 2008a). It was never clear whether the issues of consumer protection were really ever addressed, although a *Democrat and Chronicle* editorial (2008) suggested that some kind of compromise was made. Apparently part of the compromise was that Iberdrola would not raise consumer rates for a year. Four months after the Iberdrola buyout, in which the company said they would not seek rate hikes for at least a year as part of the agreement with the Public Service Commission for buying NYSEG, the company requested a 24.9 percent increase (Stinson 2009). This translates to a monthly increase for the average customer of $21 (*Leader* staff 2009). Several facts are clear: (1) NYSEG is now owned by the multinational corporation Iberdrola; (2) nearly one-fifth of New York state will depend on this company for its electricity; and (3) the electrical station on Mackey now belongs to Iberdrola.

Near the electrical station, fields of corn and soybeans with their orderly furrows roll up and down the hills. If the corn harvest follows the average trend, one-quarter of it will go for biofuel production, and the soybeans will be processed by an Archer Daniels Midland facility into oils used for a multitude of processed foods and soy meal for livestock.

Along this part of the road the wind turbines are most visible. In spring of 2008, the first wind turbines rose along Lent, Pine, and Dutch Hills. Like mushrooms, there were three, then six, then a dozen, then two dozen. The whole horizon seemed to be sprouting turbines. Each turbine began as a single metal stem, rising three hundred yards into the sky, with three blades each the length of a football field and a swing arc of nearly a tenth of an acre. They are huge. On the summer solstice of 2008, I counted thirty-five turbine stems, and by August the blades appeared on some of the turbines; by October there were forty-seven completed. In January 2009, they began to turn.

It is well documented that the companies that own these wind turbines are not local businesses, that wind developers have been heavily subsidized by state and federal government (i.e., taxpayers), that many have tried to avoid paying local school district taxes, and that their business practices are sometimes unethical and destructive to local communities. (The Conhocton Wind Watch offers news and information on some of these issues.) Two lawsuits by the Prattsburgh and Naples Central School District charging First Wind (formerly called UPC Wind) with unfair school taxes (Perham 2008a, 2008b, 2009a, 2009b) illustrate the unwillingness of these companies to pay fair taxes. Furthermore, wind developers' actions regarding land issues have revealed such a level of corruption that the New York State Attorney General's Office launched an investigation into their conduct (Perham 2008c). As a result, the state's Attorney General Office established a code of ethics targeting these companies (Staff and Wire Reports 2008). One of the events that triggered this action was the conflict of interest between the mayor of Prattsburgh and First Wind/ UPC. The mayor first brokered a land deal for the company, and then attempted to acquire access or rights-of-way for the company from landowners unwilling to sell using the process of eminent domain (Spector 2008).

The issue of wind farms has torn the community apart. When the town of Prattsburgh rescinded its agreement with the wind company, Ecogen, the company sued and vowed to fight the action (Perham 2010a). One of the company's threats was to run up the costs of legal defense to burden the town with bills they could ill afford. The legal battles continue and it is difficult to tell when the conflict will, if ever, end.

With the heavy hand of multinationals clutching the road, it might seem that Mackey would have little appeal, but amid all the signs of industry, there is still a natural beauty. When the wildflowers begin in spring, the roadside becomes a garden. In April small patches of trout lilies and trillium grow in the small hardwood grove near the southern end of the road. One year a cluster of jonquils brightened the woods near the hunting land, and clumps of nightshade like tiny lanterns livened up the ditches.

The progression of summer blooms in the sunny parts of the road goes like this: black-eyed Susans, oxeye daisies, Queen Anne's lace, chicory, trefoil, daylilies, and jewelweed. But it is later in August when the shadows grow longer that the real floral show begins. Splatters of wild bergamot (*Monarda fistulosa*) speckle the roadside and are joined by troops of other purples. Bergamot, a close relative of bee balm with its frilly ruffles, has a delicious spicy scent, and I often crush a little as a nosegay. Then come knapweed, thistle, and clover. By mid-September, the fields yellow with goldenrods and purple asters add a sporty color. Pearl crescent butterflies on black and tangerine wings flitter about the asters in much the same way that monarchs hang around milkweed.

Spring is the time when the live music begins. In March the piping of spring peepers from a small vernal pool in the woods fills the air. Poets and naturalists often use these tiny noise makers as the proclamation of spring. Maxine Kumin (2003) compares the boisterous amphibians to restless kids at summer camps, but her line "spring peepers hallow the marsh" transforms their audios into a sacred music. Dianne Ackerman (1997, 68) describes them as "thousands of electric alarm clocks beeping" and I imagine the earth being awakened by their bleeps. Joseph Wood Krutch begins and ends his *The Twelve Seasons: A Perpetual Calendar for the Country* (Krutch 1949) with spring peepers, describing their trills and shrills as the true heraldry of spring. Clearly, "nothing signals the beginning of spring . . . as emphatically as the raucous chorus of spring peepers" (Garland 1997, 25).

One spring, near the remains of an old stone cellar wall where the woods interface the field, a coyote sauntered along the edge of the newly planted cornfield. His lanky form slinked across the brown field and disappeared into the woods. Like with so many wild creatures, one is afforded only a brief glimpse. Bobolinks and meadowlarks breed in some of the hay fields, and every year the indigo buntings come back to sit on the wires like tiny blue Buddhas. Field sparrows, song sparrows, and common yellowthroats are the loudest songsters of Mackey, and a pair of red-tailed hawks nests in the woods. A northern harrier also maintains a residence; its great loopy wingspan and white rump mark is always a welcome wave.

I have watched a patch of Japanese knotweed (*Fallopia japonica*) expand from a few feet into a vast stretch of tangled greens over the years. The plant produces lacy white blossoms in spring, and in summer the dense heart-shaped leaves turn the road into a tropical hedge. Fall triggers the leaf change to rust, and in winter, when the leaves have blown away, the bare stems are the color of blood oranges. The plant, like so many things of great beauty, is seductive, and I have to remind myself not to fall for its attractiveness, but to remember it is a pest that eliminates native species. Throughout the county, particularly along rivers and in wetlands, Japanese knotweed has taken over large sections of the landscape.

Smith Pond Cemetery lies near the end of the road hidden behind a fortress of oaks. The hundred-year-old oaks surrounding the cemetery watch over the graves like sentinels. One year wild columbines grew among the stones, but the next year they were gone, probably cut by the caretaker's frequent mowing. Before the road ends at Smith Pond, a patch of brambles thick with multiflora rose, honeysuckle, hawthorns, and a few old apple trees create a warbler haven where yellow warblers, indigo buntings, and chestnut-sided warblers find a summer home. Smith Pond, with its ring of summer homes and cottages, lies at the very end of the road. Some of the residents are local folks, but many are from New Jersey, New York City, Buffalo, Rochester, and other urban areas. I sometimes wonder about these residents who have built homes in this peaceful rural setting in order to escape the city. Maybe they worked long and hard in corporations to pay for these homes; maybe they saved their money and dreamed of a cottage by a pond. The truth is, people want to escape the city and the industrial places and to live the peaceful life in rural spots, but I wonder what is becoming of our countryside?

Mackey may be a road for all reasons, but it is not a road for all people. Multinational corporations own or control much of the land along this road. And I wonder how this happened? How is it that those of us who live here do not control our own land? Why did those who once owned the land let it slip from their hands? Certainly, it may have been about economics. And perhaps it happened so slowly we were not even aware of it. The reality is we who live in one of the most beautiful regions of the world have allowed our lands to become controlled by distant corporations, and our government regulatory agents and leaders who are supposed to represent us and protect our rights seem either ineffective or handmaidens of the corporations.

One afternoon I noticed a discarded mattress and box spring in the grass along the roadside. With its splintered planks and stuffing coming out, it was a disturbing sight. How fundamental a piece of furniture, a bed. A bed like this might have ushered in our birth, eased our bodies into rest and dreams, acted as a means of finding comfort in the connection of lovemaking, and a final carriage sliding us into death. And what do we do when a thing has outlasted its usefulness. How thoughtless the person who discarded it, not to take it to the landfill a few miles away for a proper burial so its usefulness might be acknowledged in a small way or at least where its fiber and fabric might more easily blend with the earth. I wonder what will happen when the wind turbines, the electrical station, the gas wells, grow obsolete. Will the road be scattered with these as artifacts, the remains of distant economic disinterest and carelessness?

I once walked Mackey with a sense of wonder at its natural beauty; I walk it now with a growing sense of dread. I worry about the disconnection that comes when distant forces dictate, control, and turn a region into an industrial zone using the argument of energy needs and jobs. I am apprehensive about that process that seems facilitated by the collaboration of our political leaders and government officials with these interests. But more than these, I fear the loss of spring peepers, indigo buntings, and bergamot and the loss of my connection to the natural world.

10

Happy Trails

Bocek Road

Silk threads bind the bush
A master weaver in motion
Web half woven hangs

SPIDERWEBS ON A DAMP MORNING turn the woods into cut-glass crystal. The dew that collects on the silky threads transforms the fly-traps into textured glass, and I think of my grandmother's old sugar bowls. We walk Bocek when we feel the need for deep woods, because the road runs entirely through a dense forest of oaks, hickories, maples, and beeches. The woods offer a vegetable garden of colors. In spring, the foliage is celery green; in summer, it deepens to kale green. In autumn, the yellow-orange of sweet potatoes and butternut squash reign; in winter, the woods turn potato white, burnt and brown skinned.

All along the road, signs read "Wildlife Refuge," marking the land as belonging to the Bocek family. I am unsure what "Wildlife Refuge" means precisely, but I would like to think it means a place of shelter and safety for wildlife. Almost everywhere we walk, private land is posted with signs that say "Private: No Hunting, No Fishing, No Trespassing"—always "No Something"—but this sign explains why. It says "Wildlife Refuge," implying that the reason for no hunting, fishing, or trespassing is to protect the wildlife. While any landowner can establish a private park

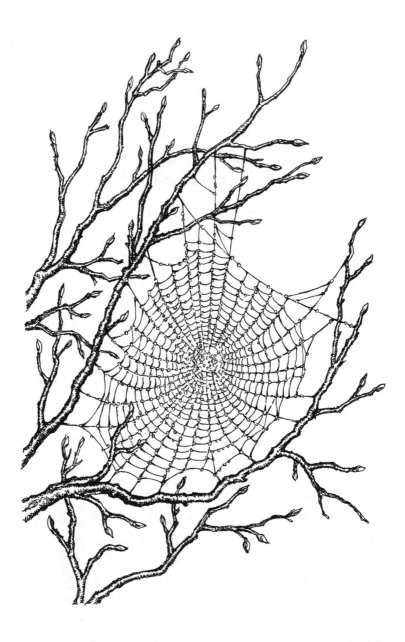

to protect wildlife by publishing a notice that it will be used as such (New York State Consolidated Laws 2008, U.S. Department of Agriculture 2011), what that means in terms of the actual treatment of wildlife is not always clear. Many private refuges have been established for hunting and hardly protect but rather keep out other hunters who do not belong to the club.

A few miles east of Bocek, a sanctuary of a different type lies cradled in the farmland hills. The place is called Farm Sanctuary, and it offers safe haven for mistreated farm animals. Founder Gene Baur (2008) describes it as home to sheep, cows, pigs, goats, chickens, and just about every other kind of farm animal. It is in keeping with New York's long and admirable history of animal protection. The American Society for the Prevention of Cruelty to Animals (ASPCA) and the Humane Society of the United States have roots in this state (Unti 2004). From well-known animal sanctuaries, like the Catskill Sanctuary founded by Elizabeth Marshall Thomas (Stevens 2009), to the small local private shelters, like A Voice for All Animals/Second Chance Ranch in Wellsburg (Kingsley 2009) run by Linda Reichel, New York has thousands of animal shelters, sanctuaries, and places of refuge for pets, farm animals, and wildlife. There is something comforting about living in a state that has so many safe places for animals.

The Finger Lakes Trail runs along Bocek for some distance then veers off downhill on an abandoned road called Sutryck toward Birdseye Hollow. The trail signs, two walkers with sticks, give me a sense of joy just as the "Wildlife Refuge" signs do. The trail is not an animal sanctuary or any sort of refuge in the truest sense, but it is a place put aside for walkers and provides access to the natural world. This remarkable footpath stretches across the southern tier of New York from Allegany State Park to the Catskill Forest Preserve (Finger Lakes Trail 2011), and has more than 560 miles of main trail with numerous branches and loops covering more than 950 miles. Founder Wallace D. Wood, known as Wally, and his trail friends held the first trail conference in 1962 and since that time, many extensions and improvements have been made (Treichler 1990). Today it is ranked as one of the finest trail systems in the United States.

Jean Rezelman (1990) recounts some of the early work on the trail. She writes about the crew's scouting adventures, of finding an ancient black walnut tree that was part of one crew member's girlhood home, and of getting lost and "crawling on hands and knees under the brush" on a deer path. She describes getting permission from landowners and all the organizations required to maintain the trail. Over the years, many individuals and groups like the Alley Cat Crew have worked on the trail creating a place that is safe and accessible and feels like wilderness. It is clearly a natural space that is cared for.

The Finger Lakes Trail has been described as a trail for people seeking outdoor adventures and a classroom for those interested in lessons in history, geology, and biology (Jensen 1992, Morris 2005). But I think of it as a pathway into the natural world. Years ago when I was younger and more sure-footed, I walked the Finger Lakes Trail, and that is where I began to appreciate the northeastern woods. My first encounter with Indian pipe was on the Finger Lakes Trail; I discovered squaw root, the vulnerable pale green orchid, sundews in marshy bogs, the lycopods or club mosses, and so many of the other less conspicuous species of the woods. I had never seen running ground pine (*Lycopodium obscurum*) or ground cedar (*L. tristachyum*), which made me think of miniature trees in toy villages, or stiff club moss (*L. clavatum*) that rises from the ground like green fuzzy caterpillars standing on end.

All those wondrous club mosses that I knew from memorizing life cycles in Botany 101 were now part of my real world. My life as a biologist encompassed four years of university course work, teaching high school, five years of graduate work, a few years of postdoctoral work, and teaching and researching for

thirty years in a university; but it was not until I began to walk
these woods that I really understood biology. I began to understand the passions of those early naturalists and nature writers; I
began to understand environmentalists and activists who write in
reverence of life; and I began to understand Buddhists. By being
in these woods, I began to see that the earth and all its life-forms
make an essential reality that I accept as my reality, and as such, I
realize how much of a true biologist I am. The Finger Lakes Trail
led me to this understanding. Just as John Donne four hundred
years ago wrote love songs to his God, I write love songs to the
club mosses and sundews.

Sundews

remind me of that old time religion—
how glitter and sweet are traps.

Still, I am attracted to their red sparkles
and would step into them if I could

giving up all that I am to a small
plant carnivore, to the sublime

knowing how little knowledge saves us
knowing what saves us is compassion.

The Finger Lakes Trail and some of the seasonal roads we
walk have a sense of rightness about them. They are not really
wilderness in the traditional sense, but they are places where wild
things live, they are accessible to almost everyone, and they offer
wondrous experiences. Like those who build sanctuaries for the
animals, the trail makers give us this miraculous pathway into
the natural world. It is that quality of generosity and compassion,
like that of the creators of sanctuaries, that offers us the gift of
enlightenment. I honor and give thanks to the trail makers.

11

In Land We Trust

Irish Hill and O'Brien Roads

The old stone fences
A touch of local color
Stop and sit a spell

IRISH HILL AND O'BRIEN ROADS make two sides of a triangle that climbs Rattlesnake Hill and passes through Moss Hill State Forest (NYSDEC 2011f). Deeply wooded and lined with old stone fences, the roads carry the legacy of the Irish families who settled and farmed the land in the 1800s. About two feet high and, in some spots, crumbling, shrunken, toppled, or sunken into the ground, old stone fences are plentiful along the back roads. Most of the stone fences of the region were made by farmers who cleared their fields every spring, perhaps wondering why stones "grew from the soil like potatoes" (Allport 1990, 59). The freezing and thawing of groundwater heaved up rocks from the soil, so clearing the fields was a constant task. While some fences functioned as animal pens, most of them marked land boundaries. The old fences provided a certain order, and townships evolved rules regarding their height, location, and maintenance (Snow 2008). A hundred years ago New York had more than 95,000 miles of stone fences (Allport 1990, 17–18). Today, who knows how many remain, but they are all over Steuben County, and we see them on many seasonal roads. Some are made from flat slate

stones and look compressed and compacted, but most are made of field stones, no bigger than could be easily lifted. These laid walls, as they are called, have a more orderly appearance than those known as rubble walls, which are composed of stones of all sizes and shapes.

Stone fences and stone walls have been considered a defining element of the northeastern landscape (Thorson 2002), and efforts to preserve them are common (Stone Wall Initiative 2008). It is no surprise that they have captured the imagination of poets and writers who have used them to honor rural life and to reveal important human truths. Robert Frost's poem "The Mending Wall" uses stone fences to illustrate the need for boundaries and order and that out of the cooperative work of mending them comes the bonding of neighbors. The classic line "good fences make good neighbors" (Frost 1973) is one that everyone recognizes. Jane Brox (1995) describes how she uses the old moss-grown, lichen-mapped fences to find her way home when she wanders the woods of her family farm. But it is Adrienne Rich who best honors life in all its magnificent complexity by using the stone fence and underlying bedrock as both setting and origin. In "Transcendental Etude," Rich sits on a stone fence and looks out over a field. She muses on the complexity of life and how short the lives of slugs, moles, spiders, even our own, "a lifetime is too narrow / to understand it all" and yet what lies underneath this teeming pattern of life is rockshelves (Rich 1978, 73). Clearly, the beauty and order of stone fences reflect the truths of life.

Also wondrous about the old stone fences are the creatures that make their homes among the rocks—especially the chipmunks who den and burrow in the nooks and crevices. They scurry over the rocks with their cheek pouches puffed out full of seeds, seemingly busy to the point of frenzy. Solitary rodents, chipmunk populations fluctuate widely from year to year, although biologists are unsure why this occurs. They live about three years, sleep deeply in winter but are not hibernators, raise young in the spring, and can be quite aggressive when defending their territory. Perched on a high point, chipmunks will vocalize or cluck like birds to mark their territory. When they bend their tails sideways, back, then forward in an S-shaped wave, they are supposedly gesturing an alarm warning. I once considered them cute, until I learned they devoured young birds and bird eggs (and apparently have a very heavy impact on songbird populations). Then they lost some of their appeal. Something about a creature's eating habits can evoke a change in their attractiveness.

On the same forested hillside, Parker Nature Preserve lies off Velie and Telegraph Roads. It does not have a stone fence, but there is a rock wall that was part of an old barn. Some of the trees growing out of it are over a hundred years old. One of twenty-six Finger Lakes Land Trust (FLLT) Preserves (Finger Lakes Land Trust 2011) and the only one in Steuben County, Parker Nature Preserve makes up part of the thirteen thousand acres, as of Fall 2011, protected by the FLLT (McLane 2004). The preserve is a small 170 acres and like all the others, it is a true nature preserve where hunting, trapping, camping, motorized vehicles, fires, bicycles, horses, and collecting are prohibited. Once an old farm, the land was donated to the FLLT by Gene and Joan Lane in 1993 and named after their grandsons, Chris and Mike Parker. A two-mile loop trail through the preserve offers an old stump-pine fence, a marsh, a pond, meadows, and both a young and a mature forest. Like much of the surrounding land, the woods of these hills are mostly red oak, ash, red and sugar maples, trembling aspen, shagbark hickory, and white birch; the conifers are hemlock and white pine. The scrubland is returning to forest, and the grasses are yielding to sumac, hawthorn, and buckthorn. Black-throated green, blue-winged, common yellowthroat, and yellow warblers as well as golden-crowned kinglets are abundant in spring along with song and field sparrows.

The FLLT, established in 1989, is a grassroots land trust supported by donations from its fifteen hundred members. More than two hundred active volunteers participate in its management; the work of Betsy Darlington has been especially noteworthy. It is a nonprofit land conservation organization whose mission is to preserve land in the twelve counties of the Finger Lakes Region. Begun by Cornell graduate student Andy Zepp as a master's project, the trust has been actively acquiring land and easements to protect it from development, mining, logging, drilling, or any of the other resource extracting and environmentally damaging activities (McLane 2009). The FLLT is not a private land conservation organization; it is not a government organization (although it has worked with certain conservation groups); it has no huge corporate sponsors, no million dollar budget or multimillion dollar assets; it is not run like a corporation; it is not used to avoid taxes nor to accumulate investments; it is a grassroots citizens' organization, in the best sense.

Pam Maurey is the Parker Nature Preserve's steward and has been for more than ten years. Her home is on a small slice of land surrounded by the preserve, and she claims "it's like having my own private sanctuary." She and her dogs, Gator and Walter, walk the preserve year round on trails she has built and maintained. She tells of encountering two large white-tailed bucks, one a ten point and the other an eight point on the trail one evening. She sat down slowly and spoke gently to them for a moment, but when they began stomping their feet and snorting, she told them they should get going now. And off they trotted (Wilmer 2004).

Another encounter involved fawns. One morning while filling the bird feeder, Pam heard loud bleating coming from the woods. She discovered two tiny fawns standing on wobbly legs, their hooves not much bigger than thumbnails. Thinking the mother would be back, she left them, but their cries continued all morning. She was able to get conservation officers to come and take the cold, malnourished babies to a wildlife rescue facility. The fawns were in such bad shape they didn't survive, but Pam uses the experience to remind her fellow FLLT members of some basic wildlife facts: "Wildlife should be left alone to care for themselves and their own" and "Surviving in the wild is not easy for young animals, but with the Land Trust there are places for them to have a chance to be forever wild" (Maurey 2001). Like the deer chronicles of Helen Hoover's classic story, *The Gift of the Deer* (1966), Pam's philosophy is that deer, like all wildlife, are not pets, but fellow inhabitants of the woods, and our relationship to them is best when tempered with respectful boundaries. Holmes Rolston echoes this philosophy when he writes in *Conserving Natural Values*, while clearly "there is somebody there behind the fur or feathers, humans must remain at a distance . . . and leave wild animals alone in their autonomy" (Rolston 1994, 101, 114).

Pam tells another story of an encounter not with deer but with deer hunters. Part of her duties as steward is to periodically send out brochures, maps, and information to the landowners who border the preserve to keep and maintain good relationships. The information is designed to reintroduce the FLLT and remind the landowners of the beautiful preserve that they may enjoy. Late one summer day, out grooming one of the trails with her dogs, three men who owned land nearby approached her. These fellows, from the northwest part of the state, were holding the preserve maps she had sent out. They were quite surprised to see a land steward. They told her they were out hiking and enjoying the preserve. It was quite obvious to Pam that they were not hikers but hunters trying to map out the best way to drive deer down off the preserve to their land for the deer season. Pam never saw them again but her presence probably saved some of the deer who live on the preserve. Her presence also preserved some important boundaries between legal hunting and slaughter.

Irish Hill and O'Brien Roads transect and border a good deal of protected land; they pass through a small state forest that borders another even larger state forest. The many thousands of acres of state forest land in the area, while not nature preserves, are certainly protected from some types of development. I remember hearing a neighbor say that her grandparents once owned some of this land and that they had donated it to the state. I imagine if the Finger Lakes Land Trust had been around, her grandparents would have donated the land to them. The FLLT's Parker Nature Preserve has been acquired by the hard work and dedication of folks who want to preserve the land and keep it as natural as possible. I have hiked several of the preserves with members of the FLLT over the years and find them to be gracious, trustworthy folks. The idea of "trust" seems to permeate their presence for not only is their organization a trust, but they have a personal trust in the land. Their motto could be, "In wild land we trust." And it is a trust in the best sense of the word, a trust in the rightness of the natural world, a trust that we can and should preserve our land because it is the honorable and ethical thing to do. When I walk Irish Hill and O'Brien Roads, I am reminded of those who believe in keeping the land wild and natural and who act on this belief. It gives me a sense of hope and trust.

12

Water, Water, Everywhere

The sun has risen
The pond an artist's palette
Landscapes ebb and flow

ONE SUMMER EVENING, I noticed a crushed plastic bottle on the roadside. The blue label read "Aquafina Pure Water, Perfect Taste." The ubiquitous hand of Pepsi Cola seems to be everywhere, I thought. I picked up the bottle and examined it closely; the label read "PWS," which stands for public water source. The source of this product, the largest-selling brand of bottled water in the world, is tap water. Pepsi Cola takes tap water, filters it, puts it in a plastic bottle, spends $20 million encouraging us to drink more water, and charges 240 to 10,000 times what it costs for that same amount of water from the faucet. Americans in 2006 paid more than $11 billion for bottled water and have spent $60 billion on bottled water since 2002: statistics cited in *Bottlemania: How Water Went on Sale and Why We Bought It,* Elizabeth Royte's investigation of the water industry (Royte 2008). Royte suggests that both the pro-bottle and the anti-bottle movements might be fashion driven while *New York Times* reporter Alex Williams (2007) writes, "Over the last fifteen years, the bottled water industry has been astonishingly successful in turning a product that once seemed an indulgence into a daily companion. Savvy marketers even managed to recast this mundane product as a talisman of sexiness." Indulgence, sexiness—sounds like Williams might have identified some of the more frivolous reasons for bottled water's success. Peter H. Gleick, however, in *Bottled and Sold: The Story Behind Our Obsession with Bottled Water* suggests that people buy bottled water for more complicated reasons: fear of their tap water, convenience, taste, and style (Gleick 2010, xi).

While the phenomenon of bottled water kind of reminds me of Tom Sawyer's flim-flamming passers-by into whitewashing his aunt's fence and believing it was cool, I think of my own behavior regarding bottled water. I once lived in Pensacola, Florida, near an area where a plume of dioxin had contaminated the groundwater. After learning the extent of this contamination, I bought the five-gallon containers of spring water. In Bath where I now live, I get my drinking water from the Fish Hatchery spring, which comes from an aquifer that runs from Keuka Lake to the Conhocton River. My tap water comes from the village. I use bottled water but try to do so sparingly and when safe tap water is unavailable. Of course, the operative word is "safe," and tap water is not always safe or reliable. I have heard people complain about the water that comes from their faucets. "My tap water smells like garbage" and "it looks like sludge" are real and legitimate complaints. Royte (2008) and Gleick (2010) discuss some of the problems with public water, such as our nation's water infrastructure not being maintained and the presence of toxicants ranging from arsenic to gasoline additives to pharmaceuticals contaminating our water supplies. Yet people vote down bills to finance updating or improving water plants because it means higher taxes. This attitude has led to easier corporate takeovers of water supplies.

Bottled water is probably as much about oil as it is about water. It takes 1.5 million barrels of oil a year to make the bottles in which this trendy water is sold, plus countless barrels to transport it (Food and Water Watch 2006). Although other products we consume generate plastic bottles, items such as soda and milk, some containerization is recognized as necessary because they do not come from the faucet. Soda bottles in New York and ten other states are recycled. In fact, 2007 marked the twenty-fifth anniversary of the New York "Bottle Bill," with the more formal name of the Returnable Container Act. Since the law was enacted, it is estimated that 90 billion containers have been recycled, container litter has been reduced by 70 to 80 percent, 2.3 million barrels of oil have been saved, and pressure from landfill space has been reduced. Unfortunately, the act did not cover bottled water, because water bottles did not exist in single-serving size when the law was passed (Kruman 2007). Like all plastic bottles, water bottles present disposal problems; unlike cardboard and other biodegradable containers, they do not decompose. Not only do these bottles stay around forever, but some leach bisphenol A, a highly toxic carcinogen (National Institutes of Health—National Toxicology Program 2008).

Some hopeful local notes regarding bottled water were that on January 3, 2008, the Steuben County Public Works Committee voted to expand the county's plastic recycling program to accept No. 1 and No. 2 plastics. Bottled water comes in No. 1 plastics. The county now sells these plastics, which go for around $400 per ton and they make about $36,000 a year in revenue (Clark 2008). Also, a new Bigger Better Bottle Bill, part of the 2009–10 New York State legislation requiring a deposit on all water bottles, went into effect in October 2009 and has resulted in more recycling as well. Every water bottle is now worth five cents.

The most troublesome issue with bottled water is the corporatization of our water (Klessig 2004). Large corporations are buying up land all over the country (and the world) for the water rights. In New York, lands with springs are especially sought after and being purchased "with the aim of developing new sources to meet the growing demand for bottled water." As a note of interest, Nestlé Waters North America, the company that bottles Poland Spring, Deer Park, Ice Mountain, and several other labels, was planning to purchase Blue Springs Farm in Orwell and take water from the Tug Hill Aquifer. In other words, Nestlé was planning to buy the public's water and sell it back to the public at exorbitant prices. The company claimed the plant would provide three hundred jobs. Nestlé dropped these plans, supposedly, from pressure by Trout Unlimited and several other environmental groups (Nearing 2009).

Small businesses are also after the bottled water dollars and are getting support from the government to do so. In nearby Avoca, a company called Avoca Spring Water (formerly Nature's Nectar Spring Water) begun bottling water in 2005. The spring and the property around the spring were purchased in 2003 and are privately owned. The company's Web site says the spring water is filtered through a one-micron filter, sterilized using UV and ozonization, and bottled in five-gallon containers. According to the Web site, "plans to produce small bottles of water for personal consumption" are also under way (Avoca Springs Water 2006). The company charges about one dollar per gallon for the large containers. In the small half-liter bottles, the water will cost over seven dollars per gallon. Imagine that, water that costs twice as much as gas or milk! A Google search revealed that the company received a $15,000 Federal Assistance Small Business loan in 2005 (OMB Watch 2005). While the company is strongly applauded by the local business community, I wonder if we can ignore the fact that it is selling water that belongs to the public. The land and the spring might be owned by the company, but the aquifer from which the water flows is a community resource. I do not know how many jobs the company provides or what it pays in community taxes (as a small business, it undoubtedly pays relatively more than large corporations). The reality, however, is that we must consider this question: What is better, a small business locally owned or a large corporation?

While I am constantly amazed at people's desire for convenience, the bottled water phenomenon is here to stay. It is the path we have decided to take and we Americans love convenience, but by doing so we are polluting the environment and creating a culture where corporations get richer using public resources. The crushed plastic bottle on the roadside, and this was not the only place I had seen such bottles, is a reality. All over the countryside, the roads are littered with these bottles, and if the predictions are correct, there may be a lot more of them to come.

At a bend in the road, cornfields on one side and grassy meadows on the other open onto a spectacular view of wooded hills and valleys. From the pinnacle, two valleys lie cradled in the hills defined by their water bodies. Lamoka Valley holds Lamoka Lake, and through the Conhocton Valley runs the Conhocton River. Unlike the glacier-carved Finger Lakes, Lamoka is a kettle lake formed by the melting of a huge boulder of ice deposited by a glacier. The Conhocton River flows down from around Springwater, joins the Chemung, then the Susquehanna, and finally empties into the Chesapeake Bay. While it may seem this is a land of water, the rain-fed aquifers are shallow and drinking water is not an inexhaustible natural resource.

At the bottom of Platte Hill, the Savona diner offers a simple menu. The diner's specials are meatloaf, spaghetti, baked chicken, scalloped potatoes, macaroni and cheese, haddock, and sometimes ham and cabbage, all for around eight dollars. The cooks have been there for years, and the waitresses always bring out large glasses of water. After a hot walk, the taste of cold water is a welcome pleasure.

One afternoon as I drank a tall cool glass of water, I wondered where this water came from. I found that until recently everyone in Savona got water from individual wells. Every home and business had its own well. But the village had just built its own water system after being awarded a $1 million grant and $3 million interest-free financing by New York State Environmental Facilities Corporation (NYSEFC is actually a public benefits organization, not a corporation) via Drinking Water State Revolving Funds (NYSEFC 2006). Many small towns and villages are deciding to build their own water systems. Jasper, for example, a small town in the southern part of the county, and Painted Post, in the eastern part of the county, are considering their own water and sewage systems.

The popular press is full of articles claiming that water is the next limited resource and its demand will make it "liquid gold." For example, in *U.S. News and World Report* (June 4, 2007) the cover article, "Water Woes," captures the dilemma: "It's a special commodity everyone takes for granted. But supply is shrinking, pipes are aging, and few are willing to pay the price . . . we have to treat it, to move it around, store it, and distribute it to homes in a process that costs a heck of a lot of money." What is happening all over the country is that corporations are moving in and buying up communities' water systems, claiming they can provide residents with water at a more reasonable cost. Communities with aging water systems or with no water system at all, especially those with small tax bases, are tempted to buy into this promise. What actually happens when corporations move in and privatize water is that the price of water goes up and the quality of water goes down. All over the United States, from New Orleans to Atlanta, Lexington to Indianapolis, the history of water privatization has been a dismal failure for the citizen (Food and Water Watch 2006; Kaufman et al. 2007). Clearly, the most crucial point in the water issues is that communities, towns, and villages make laws and enact policies that allow them to retain control of their water supply and that corporations do not take over their water systems.

One of the comforting things about living in this region of New York is that there is a strong sense of community and activism. Several groups have organized events designed to make citizens more aware of their water supply and water issues. The Finger Lakes Progressives held a "Water Rights Conference" in October, 2006, and the Steuben County Sierra Club held "Water Day" in June, 2007, 2008 and 2009. All the events, exhibits, films, brochures, and discussions were designed to inform the public about current water issues.

Around another bend in the road, a pond reflects the canopy of the surrounding maple and hickory trees. The pond is a kaleidoscope of the seasons changing from the yellow-green of spring, deep summer green, auburn in fall, and gray-brown in winter. One summer evening we watched a flock of turkeys, three adults and a dozen jakes, waddle along the newly plowed banks. That section of road running beside the pond and into the woods is heavily posted. Nearly every tree has a bright orange-red sign saying, "No Trespassing, No Hunting or Fishing." The landowner is listed on the signs as "Smith [a fictional designation], Bath, NY." We met Mr. Smith one evening when we first started walking the road. He was throwing up dust as he zoomed along the road in a big dark shiny new pickup. When he stopped, he kept insisting he was the owner of this land and asking us what we were doing and where we were from.

With a little Internet searching, I discovered that Mr. Smith lived in another part of the county and managed this land for hunting. An ad on a Web site called "NYS Hunter," part of a site "where NY state hunters unite," advertises places to hunt. It describes a 463-acre property, "Triple R Mountain Spring Farm," which could be the owner's land, as having been managed for wildlife since 1987 (NYS Hunter 2004). That may have accounted for the newly constructed and dredged pond as part of a management plan. According to the advertisement, the charge for "the finest deer and turkey hunting in the state" is $2,000–$2,500/week in the fall and $1,000/week in the spring. Triple R Mountain Spring Farm might also be a member of the DMAP (Deer Management

Assistance Program) sponsored by the state's Department of Environmental Conservation (NYSDEC 2011g). The program provides assistance to land owners who lease their land for hunting by generating income and reducing property taxes. Given that New York state property taxes are the third highest in the nation, and Steuben County ranks as the thirteenth highest taxes in the United States (Clark 2009), a property of nearly five hundred acres assessed at a million dollars might be taxed well over $10,000 per year. So I sympathized with the need for some tax relief.

But the discovery left me feeling disappointed. I had the naïve notion that the land around the road was open space, farmland and woods left for wildlife. I loved walking this seasonal road, because it has given me access to a beautiful natural place. The complaint from hunters that "there is no more open access to any land anymore" (New York Hunting Forum 2008) is my complaint as well, but their concerns have resulted in tax relief for land converted from agricultural to hunting land (New York State Bills 2008). Of course, the argument could be made that the state is encouraging farmland conversion to hunting land rather than conversion to development.

In the fall of 2007, I noticed logs piled along the roadside. The forest had been cut for timber. In the fall of 2008 trees were cut again. That summer I spotted a fellow removing stones from the mounds in the field and putting them onto wooden pallets. The stone mounds are the work of early farmers who once cleared the fields and piled the rocks all together. The wooden pallets of stones were wrapped in wire ready to be transported and sold for construction supplies. Fieldstone goes for about five to twelve dollars per square foot and is popular for building expensive homes with stone foundations, stone siding, and stone fences. I'm guessing the stones might be generating a sizable profit.

In the summer of 2009, half a dozen pickup trucks with logos reading "Precision Pipeline" and "Fortuna Energy" parked in the bend of the road. The crews were digging a pipeline across the back of the field. One crew member told me the landowner had leased the land for a natural gas pipeline; this one connected to the Sunoco Pipeline.

Mr. Smith certainly seems to be a person of great enterprise determined to use every resource the land could offer. He was following the philosophy of today which is managing the land. Leasing the land for hunting, leasing it for a natural gas pipeline, harvesting timber, selling the fieldstones, I wondered what he would come up with next. Maybe wind turbines and gas drilling leases were on his list. In all fairness to Mr. Smith, he was doing what most think as positive land management. He was providing a service by controlled hunting, an activity that lasts only several months of the year and generates tax relief, which results in retaining local control of the land.

Even though I have deep concerns about hunting, timbering, and various extraction activities, I was grateful the land along the road was not being developed for housing or industrial buildings. The fields still offered monarchs that glided like Tiffany kites through patches of milkweed, bobolinks that bubbled in the fields, redwings that twanged as they hovered above the grasses in spring, and wood mint in summer. There were mulberries and raspberry bushes and wild apples and flycatchers and kingbirds and catbirds and so many more. But I wondered for how long. It seems the more I learn about land, who owns what and what landowners do with it, the more I discover that money is the deciding factor.

The land along Platt Hill Road, like so many of the roads I walk, is not about habitats for wildlife. It is not about preserving natural habitats. It's not about a land ethic, a healthy green community, or an ecology for all. It is about private ownership and a way of generating income through commodities or tax reduction. I am reminded of Wendell Berry's description of our national character: we seem incapable of escaping the "mentality of exploitation" (Berry 1977, 7) and "Faustian economics" (Berry 2009, 26).

Sometimes I wonder in this commodity culture if everything is owned by individuals who want to use it to make money and keep you out, or by corporations who want to make money and exploit you. It may be that water will no longer be a public resource; it may become a commodity to be bought and sold. And I wonder what next, the air we breathe? Certainly, it seems, even the earth's stones are commodities. It makes me sad that in the words of Madonna "we are living in a material world" at the expense of our natural world.

13

The Pulteney Highlands

Down the dirt road see
A fox dusting its red coat
Only in summer

IN THE NORTHEAST CORNER of the county, the Pulteney Highlands provide seasonal roads that offer loops. Some of the roads overlook Italy Valley, some overlook Keuka Lake, and others run up and down the hillsides. Several cross the Drumm and the Hawk View farms with their long stretches of corn and hay fields interspersed with woods. The sign in the front yard of the Drumm's three-story farmhouse reads, "Dairy of Distinction," and it is surrounded by seasonal flowers. There are no rusty tractors sitting idly in tall grass; there are no rundown sheds; there is nothing shabby about the place. The lawn is always trimmed, and the flower gardens are full of color. Across the road the family has restored an old schoolhouse. Everything about the farm is as tidy as a completed crossword puzzle.

My walking companion's grandparents had a farm a mile or so down the road, much like my own Welch grandparents' farm in central Wisconsin. My Nain and Taid's (Welsh for grandmother and grandfather) farm was in a region of glacial moraines with a Great Lakes climate and a landscape similar to this one. Both my companion and I had childhood memories of pulling fresh

peas off the wagons on their way to the cannery and eating them raw, of climbing the old farmyard trees, of cut hay smells, and all the many pleasant sensations of a farm. Our visits were just that, visits; we never knew the hardships that were part of our mothers' childhoods. To us the farm was a place of fun and adventure. Even though I never worked on a farm and have no real experience of farm life, I admire farming just as I do any occupation that involves real labor, commitment, and a close relationship to a place. There is something fundamentally appealing about family farming, and I am reminded of Wendell Berry's decades of praise for farm life. He presents the small farm as the means of making a worthy living producing food and forming essential connections and commitments to our land (Berry 1977).

Clearly, there is something quintessential and honorable about the American farm, and the vast body of agrarian literature illustrates this. The earliest accounts of farm life as exampled by Hector St. John de Crevecoeur's 1782 *Letters from an American Farmer* and Susan Fenimore Cooper's 1850 *Rural Life* (quoted in Finch and Elder 2002) were written in a time when the writers actually made their livelihood farming, so there was an intimacy and truthfulness about the writing.

Stories of farm life in the twentieth century, and especially post–World War II, have primarily come from columnists, editors, novelists, college professors, celebrities, retired persons, and others who made their living from sources other than the farm. In the late 1940s, the best-known account was Louis Bromfield's *Malabar Farm* (1947). In the 1960s through the 1980s, Josephine Johnson (1969, 1973) writes of her Ohio farm, and Noel Perrin's *First Person Rural* series (1978, 1980, 1983, 1991) details Vermont farm life. From self-described farmers' wives, we get images of farms such as Triple Ridge Farm (Pochmann 1968), End o'Way (Leimbach 1977), and a Hoosier farm (Peden 1961, 1966, 1974). In the 1980s and 1990s, farm life is portrayed by a vast array of writers: New

Yorker Richard Rhodes (1989), who actually made his living farming, as does Amish writer/farmer David Kline (1990); Gene Logsdon (1994), whose books describe his farm in Upper Sandusky,
Ohio; and Jane Brox (1995, 1999, 2004), who weaves her memoirs
of her Massachusetts family farm with the loss of viable income
from that endeavor.

The new millennium continues the outpouring of farm narra-
tives with books by writers such as Jerry Apps (2007) about his Wisconsin farm, Richard Triumpho (2005) on his Long Island organic
farm, Sylvia Jorrin (2004) on her farm in Delaware County, and
Steve Coffman (2008) about his farm near Dundee, New York. So
many writers present the farm as a crucial place of being connected
and affirming life. The ones mentioned here represent only a few
of the many from the movement known as the new agrarianism.

The Drumm farm is not a gentleman's or gentlewoman's
farm (Steuben Spotlight 2009); it is not a showcase or a weekend
farm; it is not a tourist farm (there is actually a body of literature that describes and promotes farms as tourist destinations;
see Small Farm Center: Agritourism 2008). It is a working farm
with the family income derived from farming. It is incorporated,
however, which means it is registered as a business. Probably all
farms have to do this to survive. The farm has a cheery air of
openness. Someone is always about working either in the dairy
or in the fields and waves and acknowledges our presence. It
is this friendliness, the evidence of hard work, cleanliness, and
order that make the roads here so pleasurable. The farm is not a
nature preserve, of course, but like many farmers (Jackson and
Jackson 2002), they employ those universal practices that make
small farms ecologically and environmentally friendly and sustainable, practices such as rotating fields, using manure fertilizer
generated from the cows, and intercropping.

The farmland along the roadside is planted in corn, alfalfa,
hay grass, or clover, and throughout the year, we watch the

changing textures of the fields: dark manured soil, pungent and tangy, turns to snow covered and then to muddy melts. After plowing, the fields awaken in new green and slowly ripen to lush emerald summer green. The cornstalks wave banners, and the alfalfa whistles at the wind. The fields turn golden, then dry to flaxen, and after harvest the cycle begins again.

As tidy as the Drumm farmhouse, another old farmhouse, described as an "1890s Victorian County Home," sits on Tuttle Road (New York Bed and Breakfast 2008). It is a bed and breakfast called "Feather Tick 'n Thyme," and the owners of the home and the surrounding lands, the Kunaks, keep the place well maintained. From the road, its lacy curtains in the windows, bird feeders, an old yellow dog in the yard, llamas in the field, and a large weathered barn give the place a country inn appeal.

Woods border the fields. Oaks, hickory, maple, and beech trees interspersed with patches of evergreen make a multitextured forest. A row of hawthorn (*Crataegus* species) creates a high hedge, behind which grows young alders. Several fallow fields are overgrown with both native and nonnative shrubs. The most common, the invasive autumn olive (*Elaeagnus umbellata*) and the multiflora rose (*Rosa multiflora*), add their troublesome beauty. Multiflora rose has luscious white-briar flowers in summer and in winter the bare branches arch like an elegant fountains pouring forth red water. Gray dogwoods (*Cornus foemina ssp racemosa*) tint the fields maroon in fall, and staghorn sumac (*Rhus hirta*) accents with burnt amber spikes. One summer the long blades of a cucumber magnolia (*Magnolia accuminata*), the only native magnolia in the region, added a tropical touch to the verge.

Along Ford Road, signs read, "Posted, No Hunting, E. Poore, Prattsburg, NY." A grove of white spruce occupies the northwest corner of Baughman and Ford, their welcoming branches bottlebrush stiff. One May when the air was full of pollen, thumb-size red cones speckled the trees. The morning sun shone on them and they glowed like Christmas bulbs. Within days after fertilization, the cones lost the cherry pigment and turned green. And the trees became ordinary again.

The following month walking by the spruces, a cloud of insects rose into the warm air and covered us. They lit on our shirts, landed on our pants, and when I lifted one of them from my shoulder, I discovered it was a ladybug. Thousands of ladybugs bringing us luck! Orange with thirteen spots, they were probably the species *Hippodamia tredecimpunctata*. I had been on the lookout for the two native species, the nine-spotted (*Coccinella novemnotata*) and the two-spotted ladybugs (*Aldalia bipunctata*) since participating in collection efforts of the Lost Ladybug Project (2008).

Of the 4,500 species of ladybugs in the world, five hundred are found in the United States, and those two native species, the nine- and two-spotted, were once common in New York. The nine-spotted ladybug was and still is the state of New York's official insect. In the past twenty years, however, these two species have almost disappeared, and Cornell researchers (Lost Ladybug 2008) are not sure why or what it means. The reason so many nonnative ladybug species are now common may be because they were introduced both accidentally and on purpose to help control crop-damaging aphids. The introduced species, as in so many cases, thrive better and probably outcompete the native ones.

Biologists have studied changing species for decades, documenting the loss of native species and the increases in nonnative or invasive species, but certain ones have been overlooked. How their changes affect the ecology is even more cryptic. It is easy to observe the most obvious invasive species such as knotweed or purple loosestrife, but changes in the populations of smaller, more subtle species such as ladybugs and certain invertebrates often go unnoticed. And who knows what their disappearance means in broader ecological terms. While I have never encountered the native ladybug species, I keep looking for them.

There are several ponds along Ford, some hidden in the woods. Just beyond the hunter's cabin, near Mr. Bingamon's land, is one of my favorite spots. Some years ago, I noticed two beavers gliding through the duckweed that covered the pond. When they saw us, they quickly sank into the black waters, leaving a hole in the lacy green surface. That fall, fresh beaver chews were all over. Small downed trees with raw whittled points lay along the shore, and the stick-pile lodge on the other side of the pond grew larger. Upon seeing the beavers, I read what I could find about New York's state mammal. Muller-Schwarze and Sun (2003) give an excellent natural history of the beaver, describing the animal's life cycle, its life span of ten to twelve years, its mud-and-stick lodges, its food of inner bark and aquatic plants that gets stockpiled for winter, and its population declines. Beaver populations may have been 200 to 400 million in the United States before the first settlers, but by the early 1900s, there were only one hundred thousand remaining. In New York, the beaver was nearly extirpated in the 1800s. Conservation efforts helped populations recover in the 1900s, and according to the NYSDEC Web site entitled, "Nuisance Beaver" (NYSDEC 2011h), there were 17,500 active colonies in 1993. Although I find it troublesome that the state's conservation department still considers beavers a "nuisance," that paradox seems to be inherent in conservation. Today there are an estimated 10 million beavers.

Similar to the experience described by Louise Dickinson Rich (1962), I was unable to spot the beavers again. But I have noticed their stick-pile growing a little each year and fresh chews every fall, so I know they are still about. The beaver has been a favorite topic of naturalists throughout the twentieth century. It might be the qualities of its attachment to home (Mills 1913), its habit of constant building (Milne and Milne 1960), the animal's resilience (Lawlor 2005), or even its appearance (Kanze 2007) that have inspired such writings. Kanze (2007, 105) describes one of his local beavers, Twitchy, as having a pancake tail and formidable pumpkin-colored incisors, so who could not be attracted to such a delicious creature? Probably the most poignant works on beavers are by naturalists Dorothy Richards (1977) and Hope Ryden (1989), who write of their intimate connection to beavers. Richards chronicles the building of a beaver haven called Beaversprite Sanctuary in the Adirondacks and traces her involvement with a beaver family.

We often see red foxes in the area. One fall afternoon we watched a vixen roll in the road dust, scratch, and groom her coat. Her preening went on for some time, but when I looked away for a moment and back, she was gone, in a head-turn. Some months earlier we spotted her in a field hunting mice. She leapt up into the air, pounced on a spot, dug around, leapt again into the air, pounced, and dug again. Over and over her catlike hunt was a "leap-pounce and dig" dance, almost playfully choreographed but deadly serious in its intent.

Some of the fields along the roads provide stop-over habitats for migrating birds. One spring thousands of snow geese descended on a field and fed for several days. Small groups would lift off the cold ground, fly in loopy circles, and flutter back down. Then another batch would perform the same maneuver. Their numbers were as staggering as their noise. William Fiennes (2002) writes in *The Snow Geese: A Story of Home,* inspired by Paul Gallico's classical story, *Snow Geese* (Gallico 1941), of following the birds on their migratory route. He described their flocks as so large "there were more birds than there are words in this book." While there were not that many in this flock, they were certainly a huge and noisy crowd.

Canada geese also move through in spring and fall; their Vs drape the sky and their honks fill the air. One species not on the decline, these birds have increased their numbers in the past twenty years with populations around two hundred thousand in the state and probably a million in the Atlantic Flyway (NYSDEC 2011b). On the ground they seem rather awkward—they make me think of plump Prussian officers with white chinstraps holding their helmets in place—but in the air they are as graceful as clouds. One of the most compassionate accounts of Canada geese is Sydney Plum's *Solitary Goose* (Plum 2007), in which she chronicles her encounters with a lone goose on a pond near her New England home. Her acts of caring for the goose reconnect her to the natural world. Reflecting on the relationship between humans and animals, she weaves her personal narrative with "real geese," not metaphorical ones. She describes birds that "measure time by the quality of light; seasons, by temperature and the changing wind . . . [whose] lives are the result of millions of years of adaptation and repetition" (Plum 2007, 97). Clearly, Plum transcends the romantic or sentimental to present a respectful, empathetic portrayal of this wild bird.

In spring, the annual repertoire of the highland bird symphony begins with the twilling of swallows followed by the yodeling of bobolinks. The bobolink is the only bird "who never seems to know how to put a period to his musical sentence" (Peattie 1935, 130). With summer, the songs of yellow warblers and common yellowthroats intensify, and their duets become passionate arias. The carols of sparrows—field, white-throated, song, and vesper—add to the cacophony. One evening the music turned melancholy with the threnody of a yellow-billed cuckoo. In October, bluebirds moving through on their way south squeak little ditties, but mostly they perch on the top of the cut cornstalks in their blue uniforms and reconnoiter the fields for insects. The piercing shriek of a red-tailed hawk is one we hear throughout the year. Wild turkeys move quietly around the fields all year long, but become more visible in fall when they cluster in large winter flocks. The resident pileated and downy woodpeckers drum their presence most intensely in fall. One November, a male pheasant strutted across the road, stopped short, took one look at us, and in a manner that could only be described as sheer panic, ran for his life into the high grasses, leaving behind only the soft ruffling noise of his absence.

Gangs of crows are a constant no matter what time of year, and their calls are always the loudest. The one quality I associate with crows is noise. I don't know of any other animal except humans that makes so much noise. Biologists Marzluff and Angell (2005) claim the frenetically cacophonous displays are the hallmark of crow behavior. No other bird has executions, funerals, intricate foreplay, or such a fluid social life of competition and cooperation interwoven with noise. These wise guys have elaborate and complex improvisations and sing-alongs. Candace Savage describes the "liquid rambling medley of soft caws, coos, clicks, rattles, and grating rusty-gate sounds" as "avian Ella Fitzgerald music" and reports that song among these intelligent birds is often used to end conflicts and hostilities (Savage 2005, 82). David Quammen (2008) claims crows are bored and too intelligent for their own good, but I think they might be more like Ted Hughes's crows, poets with a full range of motives and emotions (Hughes 1971), and their songs reflect this complexity.

Walking the Pulteney Highlands, I am aware the land supports so many ways of making a living. From the work of farmers and beavers, the resident birds that gather insects and seeds and raise young, the vagrant birds that stop and feed on their way through, the red foxes and the hawks that hunt rodents, and even the innkeepers, I see that the land provides. I also see that the land is cared for: in the way landowners do not cut the forest and leave the fields as shelter to the wildlife, in the way the farmers keep the soil fertile and leave a bit of grain here and there, and in the very order of the land. From the spruce grove, the beaver pond, the crop fields, the woods, the fallow fields—all of these places illustrate the richness of a flora and fauna care.

I know that gas wells and pumping facilities speckle the region, pipelines cross the fields, and in 2008 a row of wind turbines appeared on the distant ridge. These industrial marks have touched the land lightly, but they grow more evident every year. Once this land was forest, then farmland, and now it is a rich pastoral mixture. When the first natural gas wells came, they did not heavily impact infrastructure and were not intrusive. With the coming of the wind turbines and of the drilling by hydraulic fracturing, I hear the drums of industrialization getting closer and closer. In January 2010, Chesapeake Energy proposed to use a nearby abandoned gas well for disposal of their toxic brine wastewater from natural gas drilling (Ek 2010). At a town meeting, residents, along with landowners and homeowners whose properties ring Keuka Lake, urged the board to tell Chesapeake to go away (Perham 2010b). In February 2010, the company withdrew its application because of public opposition (*Star Gazette* 2010). Although I wonder where Chesapeake will go next, my hope is that the landowners will continue to keep the highlands as free of industry as possible. It is a hopeful sign that the local citizens are trying to keep their lands and waters as free of pollution and environmental damaging activities as possible.

14

A Graceland

The snow came today
Cloaking each tree branch in white
Everywhere snow ghosts

THE OLD SENTINEL OAKS that line Holmes Road have watched the land for a hundred years. As young trees they saw the fields in potatoes, food that went directly from the land to the table. Today the fields grow corn for ethanol, feed for cattle, or soybeans for oil—crops that require processing and don't end up on the table for years or maybe not at all. I wonder if the old trees view what we do to our crops as frivolous or as a tangled web of manipulation and if they question what other complexities we will invent for the sustenance that comes from our good earth.

Pileated woodpeckers live in these woods, and their carvings sculpt the old drumming trees. One usually flies from an open field like a crow with a snappy wing beat and white spots, then latches onto the side of a tree tight as a refrigerator magnet. We hear their wild laughter loudest in spring. In fall they quiet down, but their drumming continues to echo across the fields. Excavating for ants and insects, their digs attract other birds, and we often see downy woodpeckers, red-bellied woodpeckers, and sometimes house wrens around their long holes.

The tamaracks that border Holmes put on fuzzy green sweaters in spring and sway like dancers in the warming breezes. In summer they make deep shade, but come November, they throw their needles down, turning the road into a silk carpet of gold. Slippery with gilded threads, the fall carpet has us walk cautiously. The tamarack's tangy scent mixed with the smoke of a wood-burning stove from a nearby house signals the coming of winter as accurately as a clock chiming the hour.

Where a streamlet crosses Holmes, phoebes spend the summer and red-winged blackbirds gather in the trees for afternoon group cackles. They leave when the nesting is done, but other redwings come in later. Arriving from northern Canada and filling in the space left by the others, these crimson patched groupies give the impression that they are around until snowfall. Perched in the bare trees like ripe plums, they wait until something triggers the need to fly south. Below in the cornfields, the dry flaxen stalks rattle like the crunching of brown wrapping paper. When the blackbirds are gone, the only birds that remain are the little winter toughies, the chickadees, and the juncos.

In the summer of 2008, the stems and tri-blades of the wind turbines appeared on the ridge like white Calder irises. About the same time, we noticed two men working in a field. They were present much of the summer, bulldozing, building what looked like some sort of embankment or levee, and planting a few trees. I learned they had been contracted by Ducks Unlimited to build a conservation area. With a little Internet searching, I discovered that Ducks Unlimited is a nonprofit organization (referred to as a nongovernmental organization or NGO) whose one million members are mostly hunters. According to its Web site, it is the world's largest and most effective wetland and waterfowl conservation organization and has conserved more than 12 million acres. In 2007 its annual budget was $213 million, coming from members, government, and corporate sponsors, about one-third from each group. Federal and state habitat reimbursements amount to around 27 percent; corporate sponsors include Budweiser, Bank of America, Echo (an outdoor power-equipment company), Federal Premium Ammunition, Mossy Oak (a camouflage product company), Winchester Ammunition, and United Country Real Estate.

The landowners, two real estate agents from Hornell, apparently negotiated a contract with Ducks Unlimited to build wetlands. It is unclear who would be allowed on the land after the wetlands are built—all hunters or only members of Ducks Unlimited—but the reason for the conversion of the land from field to wetlands may be more about tax breaks than conservation. The landowners probably qualify for both property and income tax breaks. Conservation Easement Tax Credit, or CETC, in New York allows anyone owning property to receive a 25 percent exemption from town, county, and school district property taxes up to $5,000 (Jordan 2006). Also available is a federal income tax deduction equal to the value of the development rights (Maker 2005) and a state income tax deduction of up to $5,000 (Hudson Highlands Land Trust 2008). So the landowners gain hefty tax advantages by building a conservation area.

In addition to tax breaks, many other conservation incentives at both the state and federal levels give individuals money for converting their land into hunting areas. One program, the Conservation Reserve Program, funded through the Commodity Credit Corporation, an agency of the United States Department of Agriculture (2008), provides annual rental payments, cost-share assistance, and three dollars per acre if people sign up with their state's hunting access program (Winkelman 2008).

While I am grateful the area is not being turned into a housing development, I wonder about our land ethics when tax-exempt conservation seems to be the alternative to development. I have to live with the fact that my tax dollars (which I like to think of as my contributions to funding my community) are given to those who turn their property into hunting land and call it conservation, but it makes me uneasy. Just as I am conflicted about the link between hunting and conservation (my idea of conservation is sanctuary), I wonder about policies that seem to me, at best cryptic, at worst somewhat deceitful. And I think actions that fall into the realm of "doing good for personal gain," are really not particularly honorable but rather self-serving. It may be practical to have such policies, but it makes me sad to think of conservation and preservation driven by tax breaks and profit incentives.

One year the fields were planted in beets, and their leafy greens gave the hillside a straggly look until they were harvested. When the field was plowed again the ground returned to a smoother brown. One generous fall day, the fellow who lives at the end of Holmes brought out a bag of apples and offered each of us one as we walked by. We rubbed them on our jeans until their skins gleamed, and their crunch followed us all along the beet fields and beyond.

Throughout the spring, summer, and fall, the ponds along the road are busy as bus terminals. Robins and grackles fly in and out, sparrows flitter in the brambles, and flycatchers work the edges where insects congregate. By November, the ponds go still and winter enters like a harsh disciplinarian. The cold and ice sculpt everything in white marble, and the land becomes as silent as a whiteout. The only things we hear are our own footsteps crunch or the crack of an iced branch. Even our breath turns to frost.

I wonder if those landowners, the real estate agents from Hornell who are building the wetlands for a hunting reserve had ever walked these roads. I wonder if they had ever really seen the beauty of this place, heard the way it speaks in different seasonal dialects. If they had ever accepted the gifts of openness this land has to give, they might have been motivated to preserve it not for credit or tax breaks or profit, but because of the wonders it offers. And they might preserve it not for hunting (it is beyond my comprehension how anyone could intentionally kill anything on this graceland) but to leave it alone, to allow the land its autonomy.

15

Home Sweet Home

Stone Schoolhouse Road

Such a strand of trees
Ravens call these branches home
Down in the hollow

THE RAVENS APPEARED as two black undulating waves against the branches. One bird cried, the other answered as they flew off—one, into the blue opening, and the other, deep into the foliage. Ravens are wary birds and with good reason. Once common in the region before European settlers cut down the forests and shot them, they have learned to stay away from people. Ten years ago, the only ravens in New York were in the Adirondacks; now they are breeding all over the state, including in Steuben County (McGowan and Corwin 2008). Their intelligence, behavior, and interactions with their own and other species have been studied extensively by biologist Bernd Heinrich (1989, 1999). He writes, "To us, home is an area where we are at ease, because we are familiar with neighbors, with local peculiarities of food and shelter, and we recognize friends and potential enemies. I suspect it is similar with ravens" (Heinrich 1989, 82). He explains that where these birds call home is variable, and that "vagrant" and "resident" are not absolute categories for them. While I am not certain of the exact location of these ravens' nest, the woods along this road are part of their home territory. The philosopher Marjorie

Grene (1995, 67) writes that "all living things are defined by where they are." I believe the reverse is true as well, that "the where is defined by all the living things." And the ravens and the woods are as harmonious and meaningful a reality as any I experience.

Stone Schoolhouse Road runs through Urbana State Forest in the region called the Keuka Highlands (NYSDEC 2011k). An old stone schoolhouse provides the road its name, and I wondered where it might have stood. Roland Bentley's compilation of schoolhouses in Steuben County through the Steuben Historical Society (Bentley 2008) would probably document its location. Like many rural schools of the nineteenth century, it might have had a cloak room, a water pail and dipper, pine benches with straight backs, and a wood-burning stove (Fox 2002). My affection for schoolhouses probably comes from the fact that I liked school and was a fairly good student. School was an avenue of safety and richness in my life and more of a well-placed doorway to the world than was my childhood home. School was a place where smart, strong women played major roles and a level of equality prevailed. Although school also had its awful characters, in the days of the innocent 1950s they were only that, characters.

I am not alone in my fondness for these buildings as evidenced by the preservation of many old schoolhouses (One-Room Schoolhouse Center 2011). Preservation and restoration of these old places are being done both physically and in memoirs. One of the strongest entwinements of schoolhouse and home comes from Mary Swander, who writes about her Amish schoolhouse home, Fairview (Swander 1995). It was her intent to create a healthy place to live and to heal from an environmental illness. She did not remodel it or fix it up to some ideal of *House Beautiful* magazine but kept it simple and functional. Her choice of an old schoolhouse, I believe, represents a choice of place that embodies the qualities of healthy, righteous living.

People have such different ideas of home. An article in the *Democrat and Chronicle* (Chao 2007) describes an all-American family. The photograph of the father with his wife and daughter flanking him reveals a prosperous family: he, the CEO of an insurance company, fifty-something, and a bit prosperously overweight; his wife, somewhat thinner and well groomed; the daughter, also a little overweight, perhaps with Down syndrome. His dream was to have a waterfront home; he worked hard and saved all his life for one, and he purchased one five years ago for a quarter of a million dollars (now worth almost a million, the article points out). What a great investment, the subtext seemed to say, and I imagined a large majority of people might be quite envious of this family.

How different from my vision of home. I do not dream of a vast manicured lawn; I dream of native plants. I do not dream of 3,500 square feet; I live in 800. I live in a modular home in a trailer park on a small lot with a large linden tree in front. The tree threatens to engulf the house with its tentacular foliage. My home was a decision that involved a lot of factors, but I think of it as modest and as environmentally low impact as I can afford. It uses the preexisting infrastructure of the village (water and electricity), and I try to live as locally and sustainably as possible. Two minutes and I am in the countryside, a rural land full of wildlife, not just game animals, but native species that once made up the ecology of the northern deciduous forest. My dream home is a place not of isolation, where I go to get away from the wicked world or to keep the world out, but one where the natural world is close and I am part of a community.

I have watched from my porch cedar waxwings come in and perch like ornaments in the bare branches of the mountain ash. Elegantly marked birds, their slate-gray breasts, Zorro masks, sun-tipped tails, and small red shoulder patches look so much more graceful than the dull pictures in the field guides. With crests like aerodynamic racing helmets, they twitter in high-pitched buzzy voices. I have seen hundreds of redpolls erupt onto my bird feeder and stuff their throat pouches with sunflower seeds. Tiny red-topped finches, they dart from linden branches to feeder in waves of feeding frenzies. I have watched tundra swans fly over in white chevrons, their long necks stretched forward and their seven-foot wingspread embracing the sky as they search for a stopover. A few of these swans stop briefly on Keuka Lake, but I have seen six or seven hundred in the Genesee Valley fields north of Dansville. I have watched the resident family of crows dunk their bread in muddy puddles, eat the soggy globs, and then fly off on black wings drawn together like eyebrows in a frown.

I have watched the maples cycle, transforming in spring from an ink sketch to red fairy wings dangled with pearls, then to purple star trees, then losing their leaves and turning back to basic skeletal. In May the small yards turn to dandelions and look as if they have been sprinkled with gold doubloons. I have watched the yellow leaves of a fall ginkgo tree begin to cascade down until the tree was completely bare in an hour, the ground below turned into a carpet of gold filigree. I have seen fireflies in the hedges light up the borders like white string lights. I have observed the hills that surround my home as an ever-changing canvas upon which the natural colors of the land are always reflected. There are more colors than I could list that sit upon those hills at daybreak, dusk, fall, spring, storms—all the different times and lights of weather and the seasons. And when a rainbow rises from the hills, I believe it and the land are the good luck rainbows promise. All these sights are part of my home.

I have such affection for my neighbors, who are mostly older folks. I love my next-door neighbor, a smart, independent elderly lady who wears a bright red hat in winter. I love the old fellow who sits in his car for hours waiting for the mail at the post boxes. I love my neighbor who plants potato vines on vertical strings in front of her porch, transforming it into a leafy room much like the feel of a tree house. I love my neighbor who watches the geese fly over and gets so excited she waves to them. I love the walkers who saunter up and down the streets, rain or shine, dependable as daybreak. I love the lady on the corner who gathers her friends on her porch on warm summer afternoons and keeps track of all the comings and goings. I love the porch sitters, the lawn mowers, the leaf rakers, the snow plowers, the corner gatherers, the dog walkers, all the busyness of the ordinary. I love my neighbor who brings me macaroni salad, homemade applesauce, and banana bread. I love the two sisters who run the natural food store a few blocks away. I love the waves, the smiles, the hellos, the small courtesies that make my world a sweeter place. All of these simple connections are part of my home.

Some people ask upon meeting me where I live, and I suspect it is not that they are particularly interested in my actual environment, but they want a clue as to my wealth and social status. A world where your wealth, possessions, and especially your house and where you live reflect your value and importance is discomforting. I have often thought of saying I live at Linden Place (naming my home after the old tree in my yard), but that attempt at humor may not be especially well received. And I have to remember that naming a place is often a way that well-meaning folks give it value. But the point I am trying to make is that showcase houses, those designed for display, are not my idea of home.

There are so many ways we define home and so many writings about home. Anthologies and collections on the meaning of home fill the presses, but one that captures the changing landscape like few others is *The Place You Love Is Gone* by Melissa Holbrook Pierson. Pierson (2006) presents a broad picture of a culture that has gone drastically wrong. She writes of land the size of a football field paved over for each five new cars made, of the loss of two acres of farmland per minute, of her home in Rockland

County, New York, where the number of farms has gone from 17,360 to 250, and of the endless Walmarts, strip malls, and developments. Her narrative is not hypocritical, a problem I experience with some writers. Frankly, there is something deceitful about nature writers who live in the Hamptons, naturalists who live on estates purchased from real estate deals, environmentalists who are wealthy oil executives, or CEOs of coal mining companies who build private nature-preserve homes.

Our relationship to our home and our land can be exploitive or based on an exploitive way of living. We often use land like we use each other, in manipulative, oppressive ways to gain wealth, status, power, or control. Our culture frequently teaches and rewards that kind of thinking and that kind of behavior. Who among us does not want the good life of wealth and material abundance? But we do not pay as much attention to the reciprocity of that process and the costs of that wealth. While there are some who treat their land and home places respectfully and responsibly and some who try to live less exploitively, most of us live on a gradient, our lives positioned on a spectrum. On one end of the spectrum lie the more obvious exploiters: owners and managers of factory farms, some companies in the agribusiness, those in the resource extraction businesses such as timber, minerals, coal and gas or oil who pollute or carry out unsustainable practices, the multinationals who in their autonomy and distance operate on profit motive alone, those in the financial institutions who drive exploitive businesses, and the heavy, frivolous consumers who support them. On the other end of the spectrum are the folks like Wendell Berry and those who make a conscious and serious effort to live socially and ecologically sustainable lives. Most of us live somewhere in between and more often closer to the exploitive end of the spectrum. Perhaps the challenge for each of us is to shift our positions, even if only a small degree, to the more sustainable end.

The woods along Stone Schoolhouse Road reverberate with the calls of the ovenbirds in summer. "Teacher, teacher, teacher" they cry, as if they, too, are lovers of school. These woods are the birds' home, and I imagine them living in a birds' state of grace. It is with gratitude I walk this state forest knowing that while it is not a nature preserve, it will not become a housing development or the site of a big-box store, (and I hope not a natural gas drilling site using hydrofracking). There will always be ground leaves for the ovenbirds' nests; there will always be insects for them to eat. I also walk with the hope that these forests will not become the source of a question we might ask someday: "What to make of a diminished thing?" Perhaps this is the true meaning of home.

Epilogue

WALKING HAS INSPIRED LITERARY LEGACIES, personal memories, epic journeys, mystical revelations, and so much more. Walking the seasonal roads of Steuben County has certainly inspired me to write about this remarkable place. Perhaps not offering the scale of mystical revelations or journeys of epic proportions, these seasonal roads have offered many sights and insights. I have learned about my home by direct encounter—and what I have learned is both wondrous and sometimes dreadful.

The region's rural character embodies the natural world while evoking the flavor of both the Midwestern heartland and New England Yankee independence. The farmlands and forest, the fields and streams, the grasslands and meadows offer a remarkable beauty. The wildlife and flora are wonders to behold. I have never lived in a place where I could be so close to wildlife and so intimate with indigenous plants. I have never lived in a place where the seasons defined the landscape in such a dramatic way.

Every road I walk offers some unique quality of the region. Some roads reveal how our land is used, how we protect our lands, how our natural habitats can be restored, how some citizens try to live sustainable lives, and how certain citizens deal with environmental and conservation issues. The flora and fauna along the roadside, the endangered species and invasive species, the geology of the area, and the history of buildings along these roads weave a rich tapestry of place. Each road presents topics commonly explored by classical nature writers and modern environmental writers.

Burleson Road, Olmstead Hill-Allis, and the roads of the Pulteney Highlands cross crop fields and pastures, offering pastoral farmlands. But the shadow of wind farms and gas drilling operations looms near. The conflict of what is practical and what we need to preserve may play out on the canvas of this landscape. My hope is that it will not be an irreversible compromise.

Culver Creek Road, which has a honey farm at one end and a hunting club on the other, illustrates how beekeeping and hunting were once activities that sustained us but are now mostly hobbies. Robie and Hungry Hollow Roads transect state forests and offer some of the wonders of the northeast forest. Bocek Road runs along the Finger Lakes Trail, a beloved regional hiking trail. O'Brien and Irish Hill roads, near a Finger Lakes Land Trust preserve, exemplify local grassroots land protectionism. These roads illustrate the ways folks try to preserve the things they care about.

Some of the roads reflect sprawl, development, and corporate impact. Mackey Road with its natural gas storage-pumping facility, electrical station, and wind farms owned by multinational corporations raises the issue of foreign control of our rural lands, and the highly contentious and controversial activity of drilling (via hydrofracking) the Marcellus Shale, probably the most potentially damaging environmental force the region faces. The road while deeply imprinted with industry still retains a certain natural beauty, but the question of how much industrialization the land can withstand without turning it into a wasteland remains unanswered. In times of high unemployment and rising costs, what compromises will be made for short-term gains? And will the local citizens bear the cost of these industries?

Urbana Road overlooks Keuka Lake with its growing number of McMansions and land fragmentation. The conflict of what we desire and what we actually need might be illustrated in the juxtaposition of luxurious, expensive homes and our diminishing wildlife. At the same time, it is these citizens who have played a major role in protecting the area from a toxic waste disposal facility. The wealthy who can afford such homes, whose actions have fragmented the land, are also the ones who have protected it. The paradox that embodies the issue of wealth and power is always with us. While contradictions are inherent in our lives and times, how we solve them and whether we consider as many people as possible in issues of place, may define us as a compassionate citizenry or an exploitive one.

From Platt Hill Road the many water bodies of the area—the lakes, rivers, creeks, and ponds—raise regional water issues. Some of the land along the road used for generating income by extracting timber, leasing for pipelines and hunting pose the question, "What is the difference between enterprise and exploitation of our resources?" Other landowners like the Treichlers of Van Amburg Road, known for their efforts at sustainable living, the PeaceWeavers and the Amish near Harrisburg Hollow Road known for their back-to-the-land and simple communal living, and the many farmers of the region, employ some of the same means of making a living (lumbering by the Amish, for example) but they have chosen to live in a closer, more responsible relationship to the land and to one another, and that may be what makes the difference. The questions—"Is it possible to live in a practical way, in a material world, and have a prosperous and sustainable future? And what choices do we have to make to have such prosperity and a healthy sustainable future?"—might be tempered with the idea that when there is a sense of care in a community, the discordance between what is practical and what is sustainable might be resolved.

Wagner and Holmes Roads reveal how some land is placed into conservation with questionable purposes. When Aldo Leopold first proposed his land ethics, I wonder if he considered that our conservation efforts would be based on tax and investment incentives.

Finally, Stone Schoolhouse Road affords a ramble on the meaning of home. Home may be a showcase, a display of affluence and rank, a place of value, but when it is a place that is loved, it is out of that quality the most appropriate forms of responsibility are generated.

The roads' narrative celebrates and honors the rural nature and regionalism of place—the place I call home. Its local color illustrates the ways we connect to place, to our environment, and to each other. And while the details are regional, the issues particular to Steuben County are our national issues as well. It is my hope that the good people of the region whose compassion and wisdom have created this wondrous place will prevail and that the region's history of hardworking individualism, the striving for culture and intellectual growth, and the pursuing of a safe and healthy environment will continue.

References

Index

References

Ackerman, Diane. 1997. *A Slender Thread: Rediscovering Hope at the Heart of Crisis*. New York: Random House.

——. 2009. *Dawn Light: Dancing with Cranes and Other Ways to Start the Day*. New York: Norton.

Alexander, Deborah. 2007. "Sparkling Year at Dr. Frank's." *Star-Gazette*. Aug. 17.

Allport, Susan. 1990. *Sermons in Stone: The Stone Walls of New England and New York*. New York: Norton.

Andhara, Aurielle, and Bill Sitkin. 2008. *Rural Impact: What to Expect from the Gas Industry* [Documentary]. http://www.tiogagaslease.org /environment.html.

Apps, Jerry. 2007. *Living a Country Year: Wit and Wisdom from the Good Old Days*. New York: Voyageur Press.

Arthur, Chris. 2009. *Words of the Grey Wind: Family and Epiphany in Ulster*. Belfast, Ireland: Blackstaff Press.

Avoca Spring Water. 2006. http://www.avocawater.com.

Bass, Rick. 2006. "Her First Elk." In *The Lives of Rocks: Stories*, 27-45. New York: Houghton Mifflin.

Baur, Gene. 2008. *Farm Sanctuary: Changing Hearts and Minds about Animals and Food*. New York: Simon and Schuster.

Beebe, C. William. 1906. *The Log of the Sun: A Chronicle of Nature's Year*. Garden City, N.Y.: Garden City Publishing Co.

Bentley, Roland. 2008. "One-Room School Project." *Steuben Echoes* 34., no. 4: 14.

Beresford-Kroeger, Diana. 2003. *Arboretum America: A Philosophy of the Forest*. Ann Arbor: Univ. of Michigan Press.

Berry, Wendell. 1977. *The Unsettling of America: Culture and Agriculture.* San Francisco: Sierra Club Books.

———. 2009. "Faustian Economics." In *The Best American Essays-2009,* edited by Mary Oliver, 26-36. Boston: Houghton Mifflin.

Bird Conservation. 2008. "Wild Turkey: An American Success Story." American Bird Conservancy. Winter 2008/2009 issue. p. 22.

Bishop, Elizabeth. 1995. "A Cold Spring." In *The Complete Poems-1927-1979,* 55. New York: The Noonday Press.

Black Mountain College Project/Biographies. 2004. http://www.bmc project.org/biographies.htm.

Bonta, Marcia. 1991. *Appalachian Spring.* Pittsburgh: Univ. of Pittsburgh Press.

———. 1999. *Appalachian Summer.* Pittsburgh: Univ. of Pittsburgh Press.

Borland, Hal. 1957. *This Hill, This Valley.* New York: Simon and Schuster.

Bowers, William L. 1974. *The Country Life Movement in America: 1900–1920.* Port Washington, N.Y.: Kennikat Press.

Braunstein, Mark Mathew. 1996. "U.S. Roads Kill a Million a Day." *Culture Change/Sustainable Energy Institute* 8. http://culturechange.org /issue8/roadkill.htm.

Briggs, Tyler. 2010a. "Developer Woes Halt Howard Windfarm." *The Courier.* April 18, 1.

———.2010b. "Wind Turbines Will Be Built in Howard." *The Courier.* March 21, 2.

Brink, Helen K. 2009. *Steuben County Cemeteries! Good, Bad, and Gone.* Bath, N.Y.: Steuben County Historical Society.

Bromfield, Louis. 1947. *Malabar Farm.* New York: Harper and Brothers.

Brox, Jane. 1995. *Here and Nowhere Else: Late Seasons of a Farm and its Family.* Boston: Beacon Press

———. 1999. *Five Thousand Days Like This One: An American Family History.* Boston: Beacon Press.

———. 2004. *Clearing Land: Legacies of the American Farm.* New York: North Point Press.

Bryant, William Cullen. 1800. "Robert of Lincoln" http://www.bartley .com/42/747.html.

Burke, D. J. 2008. "Effects of *Alliaria petiolate* (Garlic Mustard: Brassicaceae) on Mycorrhizal Colonization and Community Structure in Three Herbaceous Plants." *American Journal Botany* 95: 1416–25.

Burroughs, John. 1871. *Wake-Robin*. New York: Hurd and Houghton.

———. 1887. *Birds and Bees: Essays*. Boston: Houghton Mifflin.

———. 1906. "Bobolonk." In *Bird and Bough*, 42. Boston: Houghton Mifflin.

Carrighar, Sally. 2002. "The Weasel." In *At Home on This Earth: Two Centuries of U.S. Women's Nature Writing*, edited by Lorraine Anderson and Thom S. Edwards, 196–98. Lebanon, N.H.: Univ. Press of New England.

Carroll, David M. 2004. *Self-Portrait with Turtle: A Memoir*. Boston: Houghton Mifflin.

———. 2009. *Following the Water: A Hydromancer's Notebook*. Boston: Houghton Mifflin.

Chao, Mary. 2007. "Hot Properties? Try Lake Homes." *Democrat and Chronicle*. July 22.

Chaskey, Scott. 2005. *This Common Ground: Seasons on an Organic Farm*. New York: Viking Press.

Clark, Bob. 2008. "Steuben County DPW to Recycle Common Types of Plastic Wastes." *The Courier*. Jan. 13.

———. 2009. "Steuben Ranks Unlucky 13 in National Tax Bills." *The Evening Tribune-Hornell*. Sept. 27.

Clark, Christopher. 2003. "The Potato Chip Is 150 This Year." Snack Food Association. http://www.sfa.org/potato150.aspx.

Coffman, Steve. 2008. *Chicken Justice: And Other Unexpected Lessons in Country Living*. New York: Hearst Books.

Cook, Elizabeth. 1973. "The Vascular Plants of Moss Lake Sanctuary, Allegany County, NY." *Science Studies*. St. Bonaventure Univ. 29: 6–43.

Cornell University Extension Newsletter. 2006. 4, no. 1 (Jan./Feb.): 4. http://www.putknowledgetowork.com/Documents/SpotlightJan Feb06.pdf.

The Courier. 2008. "New York Potato Production Rises." Nov. 16, 5.

———. 2009. "Organic Farm Offers Ways to Save." March 15.

Couturier, Lisa. 2005. "For All the Girls Who Couldn't Walk into the Woods." In *The Hope of Snakes: And Other Tales from the Urban Landscape*, 46–57. Boston: Beacon Press.

The Crooked Lake Review. 2008. http://www.crookedlakereview.com.

Deinlein, Mary. 1997. "Bobolink. The Prairie Home Companion." Smithsonian Migratory Bird Center. http://nationalzoo.si.edu/migratory birds/featured_birds/default.cfm?=Bobolink.

Democrat and Chronicle. 2007. "Thruway Truckers Balk at Toll Rise." Dec. 11.

———. 2008. "Iberdrola Ruling." Aug. 27.

Dewdney, A. K. 1998. *Hungry Hollow: The Story of a Natural Place.* New York: Springer Verlag.

Dillard, Annie. 2002. Living Like a Weasel. In *Nature Writing: The Tradition in English*, edited by Robert Finch and John Elder, 876–79. New York: Norton.

Earthworks. 2006. Hydraulic Fracturing 101. http://www.earthworks action.org/FracingDetails.cfm.

EcoBooks. 2008. http://www.ecobooks.com.

Ek, Derrick. 2010. "Wastewater Facility Proposed Near Keuka." *The Leader.* Jan. 17.

El Paso. 2008. http://www.elpaso.com.

Environmental Protection Agency. 2003. *Manual Gravel Roads: Maintenance and Design Manual.* http://www.epa.gov/owow/nps/gravel roads.

———. 2009. *Source Water Protection Practices Bulletin: Managing Highway Deicing to Prevent Contamination of Drinking Water.* #816-7-09-008. http://www.epa.gov/safewater/sourcewater/pubs/fs_swpp_deicing highways.pdf.

Faulkner, William. 1994. *Big Woods: The Hunting Stories.* 1955. Reprint New York: Vintage.

Feulner, Jason. 2007. "Party at Bully Hill." Aug. 21. *Lenndevours* http://lenn thompson.typepad/com/lenndevours/2007/08/crazy-times-at- .html.

Fiennes, William. 2002. *Snow Geese: A Story of Home.* New York: Picador.

Finch, Robert. 1983. *The Primal Place.* New York: Norton.

Finch, Robert, and John Elder. 2002. *Nature Writing: The Tradition in English*. New York: Norton.

Finger Lakes Land Trust. 2011. http://fllt.org/protected_lands/protected_lands1.php?id=36.

Finger Lakes Trail. 2001–8. http://www.fingerlakestrail.org.

Food and Water Watch. 2006. "Faulty Pipes." http://www.foodandwaterwatch.org/water/pubs/reports/faulty-pipes/?searchterm=faulty%.

Fox, Grace S. 2002. "The Rural Schools of the Town of Avoca." Part II. *The Crooked Lake Review*. http://www.crookedlakereview.com/articles/101_135/122winter2002/122fox.html.

Frost, Robert. 1973. "The Mending Wall." http://writing.upenn.edu/~afilreis/88/frost-mending.html.

Gallagher, Jay. 2008a. "Iberdrola Accepts PSC Terms for Buyout." *Democrat and Chronicle*. Sept. 11.

———. 2008b. "Iberdrola Deal Questioned." *Democrat and Chronicle*. Aug. 21.

Gallico, Paul. 1941. *The Snow Geese*. New York: Knopf.

Garland, Mark S. 1997. *Watching Nature: A Mid-Atlantic Natural History*. Washington, D.C.: Smithsonian Institution Press.

Garreau, Joel. 2007. "Honey, I'm Gone: Abandoned Beehives Are a Scientific Mystery and a Metaphor for Our Tenuous Time." *Washington Post*, June 1 http://www.washingtonpost.com/wp-dyn/content/article/2007/05/31/AR2007053102355.html.

Gleick, Peter H. 2010. *Bottled and Sold: The Story Behind Our Obsession With Bottled Water*. Washington, D.C.: Island Press.

Gooch, Bernard. 1950. *The Strange World of Nature*. New York: Thomas Y. Crowell Company.

Greater Tater. 2008. A Case Family Company. http://www.greatertater.com.

Grene, Marjorie. 1995. *A Philosophical Testament*. Chicago: Open Court.

Gutfreund, Owen. 2004. *Twentieth-Century Sprawl: Highways and the Reshaping of the American Landscape*. Oxford, England: Oxford Univ. Press.

Halfman, John D., and Kerry O'Neill. 2009. *Water Quality of the Finger Lakes, New York: 2005–2008*. Finger Lakes Institute. Hobart and

William Smith Colleges. http://fli.hws.edu/pdf/Halfmanreport05 -08.pdf.

Hamill, Sean D. 2007. "Pennsylvania Political War over Planned Tolls on I-80." *The New York Times*. Aug. 26, National Report, 12.

Harmon, John E. 2008. "Atlas of Popular Culture in the Northeast United States: Potato Chip." http://www.geography.ccsu.edu/harmonj /atlas/potchips.htm.

Harper, Karen. 1996. *Dark Road Home*. Don Mills, Ontario: MIRA.

Haughney, Christine. 2011. "As the Tolls Keep Rising, Some Still Pay Nothing." *The New York Times*. Aug. 19, A20.

Heat-Moon, William Least. 1982. *Blue Highways: A Journey into America*. Boston: Little, Brown.

Heinrich, Bernd. 1989. *Ravens in Winter*. New York: Summit Books.

———. 1997. *The Trees in my Forest*. New York: Cliff Street Books.

———. 1999. *Mind of the Raven: Investigations and Adventures with Wolf-Birds*. New York: Cliff Street Books.

———. 2003. *Winter World: The Ingenuity of Animal Survival*. New York: HarperCollins.

Hemingway, Ernest, and Seán Hemingway. 2003. *Hemingway on Hunting*. New York: Scribner.

Hersey, Jean. 1967. *The Shape of a Year*. New York: Scribner's.

Hess, Paul. 2007. "Nuthatches Understand Chickadees' Language." *Birding* 39, no. 6(Nov./Dec.): 39.

Hoover, Helen. 1966. *The Gift of the Deer*. New York: Knopf.

———. 2003. "Two Creatures of the Long Shadowed Forest." In *Sisters of the Earth: Women's Prose and Poetry About Nature*, edited by Lorraine Anderson, 228–33. New York: Vintage Books.

Horn, Tammy. 2005. *Bees in America: How the Honey Bee Shaped a Nation*. Lexington: Univ. Press Kentucky.

House, Kirk W., and Charles R. Mitchell. 2008. *Finger Lakes (Postcard History: New York)*. Mount Pleasant, S.C.: Arcadia Publishing.

Houston, Pam, ed. 1994. *Women on Hunting*. Hopewell, N.J.: Eco Press.

Hubbell, Sue. 1983. *A Country Year: Living the Questions*. New York: Harper and Row.

———. 1988. *A Book of Bees: And How to Keep Them*. Boston: Houghton Mifflin.

Hudson Highlands Land Trust. 2008. "Conservation Easement." http://www.hhlt.org/conservation.htm.

Hughes, Ted. 1971. *Crow: From the Life and Songs of the Crow*. New York: Harper and Row.

Hugill, Peter J. 1981. *The Elite, the Automobile, and the Good Roads Movement in New York: The Development and Transformation of a Technological Complex, 1942–1913*. Syracuse Geography Discussion Paper Series. Dept Geography, Syracuse University, Syracuse, N.Y. http://openlibrary.org/books/OL3850113M/The_elite_the_automobile_and_the_good_roads_movement_in_New_York.

Hyypio, Peter, and Edward Cope. 2006. "Giant Hogweed. *Heracleum mantegazzianum*." *Cornell Extension Publication Bulletin*, no. 123.

Jackson, Dana, and Laura L. Jackson, eds. 2002. *The Farm as Natural Habitat: Reconnecting Food Systems with Ecosystem*. Washington, D.C.: Island Press.

Jensen, Leona. 1992. *Retreat to the Finger Lakes: Exploring the Finger Lakes for Rest, Relaxation and Renewal*. Penn Yan, N.Y.: Chapel Street Publishing.

Johnson, Josephine W. 1969. *The Inland Island*. New York: Simon and Schuster.

———. 1973. *Seven Houses: A Memoir of Time and Place*. New York: Simon and Schuster.

Jordan, Henrietta. 2006. "Frequently Asked Questions about New York's Conservation Easement Tax Credit: A Guide for Landowners and Land Trusts." http://clctrust.org/pdf/CETC-FAQ.pdf.

Jorrin, Sylvia. 2004. *Sylvia's Farm: The Journal of an Improbable Shepherd*. New York: Bloomsbury.

Kanze, Edward. 2007. *Over the Mountain and Home Again: Journeys of an Adirondack Naturalist*. Utica, N.Y.: Nicholas K. Burns Publishing.

Kappel-Smith, Diana. 1979. *Wintering*. Boston: Little, Brown.

Kauffman, Bill. 2006. *Look Homeward America: In Search of Reactionary Radicals and Front Porch Anarchists*. Wilmington, Del.: Intercollegiate Studies Institute.

Kaufman, Deborah, Alan Snitow, and Michael Fox. 2007. *Thirst: Fighting the Corporate Theft of Our Water*. San Francisco: Wiley.

Kaza, Stephanie. 1993. *The Attentive Heart: Conversation with Trees*. New York: Fawcett Columbine.

Kenyon, Jane. 1996. "Deer Season." *Otherwise: New and Selected Poems*. St. Paul, Minn.: Graywolf Press.

Kerouac, Jack. 1957. *On the Road*. New York: Viking Press.

Keuka Lake Association. 2008. http://www.keukalakeassoc.org.

Kieran, John. 1950. *Footnotes on Nature*. Garden City, N.Y.: Garden City Publishing Co.

King, Carolyn M., and Roger A. Powell. 2006. *The Natural History of Weasels and Stoats: Ecology, Behavior and Management*, 2nd ed. Oxford: Oxford Univ. Press.

Kingsley, Jennifer. 2008. "State Urged Not to Stifle Gas Drilling." *Star-Gazette*. Nov. 14.

———. 2009. "Fundraiser to Aid Woman's Effort to Rescue Animals." *Star-Gazette*. Feb. 7.

Kirchner, W., and W. Towne. 1994. "The Sensory Basis of the Honeybee's Dance Language." *Scientific American* 270, no. 6: 74–80.

Kirk, Andrew. 2007. *Counterculture Green: The Whole Earth Catalog and American Environmentalism*. Lawrence: Univ. Press of Kansas.

Klees, Emerson. 2008. *Wineries of the Finger Lakes: The Heart of New York State*. Rochester, N.Y.: Friends of the Finger Lakes Publishing.

Klein, A. M. 1990. "The Mountain." In *A. M. Klein: Complete Poems*, edited by Zailig Pollock, vol. 2, 689–90. Toronto: Univ. Toronto Press. http://www.poetryfoundation/org/poem/172250.

Klein, Daniel B., and John Majewski. 1992. "Economy, Community, and the Law: The Turnpike Movement in New York, 1797–1845." *Law and Society Review*. 26, no. 3: 469–512. http://www. uctc.net/papers/076 .pdf.

———. 1994. "Plank Road Fever in Antebellum America: New York State Origins." *New York History*. Jan.: 39–65.

Klessig, Lance. 2004. "Bottled Water Industry." http://academic.ever green.edu/g/grossmaz/klessill.

Kline, David. 1990. *Great Possessions: An Amish Farmer's Journal*. San Francisco: North Point Press.

Klinkenborg, Verlyn. 2003. *The Rural Life*. Boston: Little Brown.

Kolbert, Elizabeth. 2007. "Stung: Where Have All the Bees Gone?" *The New Yorker*. Aug. 6, 52–59.

Krauss, Clifford. 2008. "There's Gas in Those Hills." *New York Times*. April 8. http://www.nytimes.com/2008/04/08/business/08gas.html ?_r1&pagewanted=all.

Kruman, Jennifer. 2007. "Bottle Bill at 25: Law Celebrates Remarkable Success." *New York State Conservationist* 62, no. 1: 20–21.

Krutch, Joseph Wood. 1949. *The Twelve Seasons: A Perpetual Calendar for the Country*. New York: William Sloane Associates.

———. 1969. *The Best Nature Writing of Joseph Wood Krutch*. New York: Morrow.

Kumin, Maxine. 1997. "Woodchucks." In *Selected Poems, 1960–1990*. 80. New York: Norton.

———. 2003. "Tonight." In *Bringing Together: Uncollected Early Poems. 1958–1988*. 20. New York: Norton.

Lawlor, Laurie. 2005. *This Tender Place: The Story of a Wetland Year*. Madison: Univ. Wisconsin Press.

The Leader. 2008. "Commissioner Buley Resigns." Aug. 28.

The Leader Staff. 2009. "Winner Fights NYSEG Rate Hike." *The Leader*. Jan. 31.

Leimbach, Patricia Penton. 1977. *All My Meadows*. Englewood Cliffs, N.J.: Prentice Hall.

Levin, Ted. 1987. *Backtracing: The Way of a Naturalist*. White Water Junction, Vt.: Chelsea Green.

Lewis, Beverly, and David Lewis. 2001. *Sanctuary*. Minneapolis: Bethany House.

Lewis, Michael. 2009. "The Mansion: A Subprime Parable." In *The Best American Essays–2009*, edited by Mary Oliver and Robert Atwan, 73–86. Boston: Houghton Mifflin.

Liebmann, David. 2008. "Searching for the Muse: A Survey of American Bird Poetry, 1659–2008." *Birding* 40, no. 4: 54–61.

Logan, Ben, George Vukelick, Jean Feraca, Norbert Bleu, and Bill Stokes (photographs Bob Rashid). 1995. *Wisconsin's Rustic Roads: A Road Less Traveled.* Wisconsin Rapids: MCM-Home Brew Press.

Logan, William Bryant. 2005. *Oak: The Frame of Civilization.* New York: Norton.

Logsdon, Gene. 1994. *The Contrary Farmer.* Post Mills, Vt.: Chelsea Green.

Loomis, Mildred. 1992. *Ralph Borsodi, Reshaping Modern Culture: The Story of the School of Living and Its Founder.* Cochranville, Penn.: School of Living.

———. 2008. Ralph Borsodi's Principles for Homesteaders. http://www.cooperativeindividualism.org/loomis_borsodi_bio.html. (Reprinted from *Land and Liberty,* 1978)

Lopez, Barry. 1990. *Crow and Weasel.* New York: Farrar, Straus and Giroux.

Lost Ladybug Project. 2008. http://hosts.cce.cornell.edu/ladybeetles.

Lowell, Amy. 1912. "The Green Bowl." In *A Dome of Many Coloured Glass,* Boston: Houghton Mifflin.

Lowell, Robert. 1959. "Skunk Hour." In *Life Studies.* New York: Farrar, Straus, and Cudahy. http://www.poemhunter.com/poem/skunk-hour.

Maeterlinck, Maurice. 2008. *The Intelligence of Flowers.* 1906. Reprint. Albany: SUNY Press.

Main, Walter. 2005. "The Cherry Valley Turnpike." *The Crooked Lake Review* Summer 167–71. http://www.crookedlakereview.com/articles/136_167/136summer2005/136palmer.html.

Maker, Elizabeth. 2005. "Donations That Preserve Land Forever." *The New York Times.* Aug. 14.

Martin, S. G., and T. A. Gavin. 1995. "Bobolink (*Dolichonyx orryzivorus*)." In *The Birds of North America,* no. 176, edited by A. Poole and F. Gill, 24. Philadelphia, Washington, D.C.: The Academy of Natural Sciences, The American Ornithologists' Union.

Marzluff, John M., and Tony Angell 2005. *In the Company of Crows: Crows and Ravens.* New Haven: Yale Univ. Press.

Maurey, Pamela. 2001. "Nature Preserve Update: Abandoned Fawns." *The Land Steward: Newsletter of the Finger Lakes Land Trust* 13, no. 4: 7.

McGowan, Kevin, and Kimberly Corwin. 2008. *The Second Atlas of Breeding Birds in New York State.* Ithaca: Cornell Univ. Press.

McKibben, Bill. 2006. "Small Change: Of Mites and Men." *Orion*. July /Aug. www.oriononline.org/index.phb/articles/175.

McLane, Eben. 2004. "A Walk through the Parker Nature Preserve." *The Land Steward: Newsletter of the Finger Lake Land Trust* 16, no. 2: 3.

———. 2009. "Birth of the Finger Lakes Land Trust: The Early Years: 1988–1993." *The Land Steward: Newsletter of the Finger Lakes Land Trust* 21, no. 1: 4.

McMaster, Guy H. 1853. *History of the Settlement of Steuben County, New York*. Bath, N.Y.: R. S. Underhill and Co.

Merrill, Arch. 1954. *Southern Tier*, vol. 1. New York: American Book-Stratford Press.

Miller, Cathleen. 2002. *The Birdhouse Chronicles: Surviving the Joys of Country Life*. Guilford, Conn.: The Lyons Press.

Mills, Enos. 1913. *In Beaver World*. Boston: Houghton Mifflin.

Milne, Lorus J., and Margery Milne. 1960. *The Balance of Nature*. New York: Knopf.

Moore, Kathleen Dean. 2003. "Landing." In *Coming to Land in a Troubled World: Essays*, edited by Peter Forbes, Kathleen Dean Moore, Scott Russell Sanders, and Helen Whybrow. San Francisco: Trust for Public Land.

———. 2004. *Pine Island Paradox: Making Connections in a Disconnected World*. Minneapolis: Milkweed.

Moore, Marianne. 1967. "The Wood-weasel." *The Complete Poems of Marianne Moore*. New York: Macmillan.

Morgan, Ann. 1930. *Field Book of Ponds and Stream: An Introduction to the Life of Freshwater*. New York: Putnam.

Morris, John. 2005. "The Finger Lakes Trail: Three Decades Later." *New York State Conservation Magazine*. Aug.

Muldoon, Paul. 2007. "Turkey Buzzards." *Horse Latitudes: Poems*. New York: Farrar, Straus and Giroux.

Muller-Schwarze, Dietland, and Lixing Sun. 2003. *The Beaver: Natural History of a Wetlands Engineer*. Ithaca: Cornell Univ. Press.

Murray, Jeff. 2009. "Agriculture in the Twin Tiers: Organic Farm Plants Seeds of Wellness: Bath Facility Allows People to Try a Simpler Life. *Star-Gazette*. April 13.

Nadkarni, Nalini M. 2008. *Between Earth and Sky: Our Intimate Connections to Trees*. Berkeley: Univ. of California Press.

National Institutes of Health–National Toxicology Program. 2008. "Bisphenol A." http://www.niehs.NIH.gov/chemicals/bisphenol /bisphenol.html.

National Wild Turkey Federation. 2010. http://www.nwtf.org.

Nearing, Brian. 2009. "Bottled Water Plan Shelved." *Times Union*. March 15.

Nearing, Helen, and Scott Nearing. 1954. *Living the Good Life: How to Live Sanely and Simply in a Troubled World*. New York: Schocken Books.

Nelson, Mac. 2008. *Twenty West: The Great Road Across America*. Albany: SUNY Press.

New York Bed and Breakfast List. 2008. "Feather Tick 'n Thyme." http:// www.bbnyfingerlakes.com.

New York Highway Law. 1975. Article 8. Town Highways. 205-a. Seasonal Limited Use Highway. http://public.leginfo.state.ny.us.

New York Hunting Forum. 2008. http://www.empirehunting.com /forum.

New York State Bills. 2008. http://www.assembly.state.ny.us/leg/?qs= agricultural.

New York State Consolidated Laws 2008. http://www.nysorva.org /documents/utlawsTitle3Article9.htm.

New York State Department of Environmental Conservation. 2011a. "Birdseye Hollow State Forest." http://www.dec.ny.gov/lands/37 725.html.

———. 2011b. "Canada Geese." http://www.dec.ny.gov/animals/34434 .html.

———. 2011c. "Commissioner's Testimony at NYS Assembly Hearing on Oil and Gas Drilling October 2011." http://www.dec.ny.gov /energy/47910.html.

———. 2011d. "History of State Forest Program." http://www.dec.ny .gov/lands/4982.html.

———. 2011e. "Marcellus Shale." http://www.dec.ny.gov/energy/46288 .html.

———. 2011f. "Moss Hill State Forest." http://www.dec.ny.gov/lands/37466.html.

———. 2011g. "New York's Deer Management Program." http://www.dec.ny.gov/animals/7211.html.

———. 2011h. "Nuisance Beaver." http://www.dec.ny.gov/animals/6992.html.

———. 2011i. "Pigtail Hollow State Forest." http://www.dec.ny.gov/lands/37459.html.

———. 2011j. "Timber Theft." http://www.dec.ny.gov/lands/38969.html.

———. 2011k. "Urbana State Forest." http://www.dec.ny.gov/lands/37442.html.

———. 2011l. "Wild Turkey/Turkey Conservation." http://www.dec.ny.gov/animals/7062/html.

New York State Environmental Facilities Corporation. 2006. "State Provides $11.6 Million to Campbell, Savona, Milo for Drinking Water Projects." http://nysdher.gov/Publications/ConsolidatedPlan/ConPlan.pdf.

Nice, Glenn, Bill Johnson, and Tom Bauman. 2004. "The Infamous Hogweed." Purdue Extension-WS-32-W. http://www.btny.purdue.edu/weedscience/2004/articles/gianthogweed04.pdf.

NYS Hunter. 2004. http://www.nyshunter.com/viewland.php.

Oliver, Mary. 2004. "Skunk Cabbage." In *Blue Iris*. Boston: Beacon Press. http://www.poemhunter.com/best-poems/mary-oliver/skunk-cabbage.

OMB Watch. 2005. FedSpending.org, a Project of OMB Watch: Assistance to Recipients in New York, 29. http://www.fedspending.org/faads/faads.php?&recipient_cd=NY29&fiscal_year=2005&record_num=all&detail+0&datype=1.

One-Room Schoolhouse Center. 2011. http://oneroomschoolhousecenter.weebly.com/index.html.

Palmer, Richard. 2005. "The Cherry Valley Turnpike." *The Crooked Lake Review* Spring, 101–3. http://www.crookedlakereview.com/articles/101_135/135spring2005/135palmer.html.

PeaceWeavers. 2008. http://peaceweavers.com.

Peattie, Donald Culross. 1935. *An Almanac for Moderns*. New York: Putnam.

———. 1950. *A Natural History of Trees of Eastern and Central North America*. Boston: Houghton Mifflin.

Peden, Rachel. 1961. *Rural Free: A Farmers Wife's Almanac of Country Living*. New York: Knopf.

———. 1966. *The Land, the People*. New York: Knopf.

———. 1974. *Speak to the Earth: Pages from a Farmwife's Journal*. New York: Knopf.

Pennsylvania State University. 2000. Center for Dirt and Gravel Road Studies. "Better Roads, Cleaner Streams." http://www.dirtandgravel.psu.edu.

Perham, Mary. 2008a. "First Wind to Start Building in Spring. *The Leader*. Aug. 11.

———. 2008b. "Officials Hope New Weapon Works in the Fight against Milfoil." *The Leader* April 8.

———. 2008c. "Wind Developers under Investigation. *The Leader*. July 16.

———. 2009a. "Deal Reached on Wind Project: Tax Incentives Still Awaits Approval from School District." *The Leader*. Jan. 23.

———. 2009b. "Sales Tax Revenues Down." *The Leader*. Jan. 31.

———. 2010a. "Hot Air Still Swirling over Windfarm Ruling." *The Courier*. Dec. 5.

———. 2010b. "Pulteney to Chesapeake: Go Away!" *The Courier*. Feb. 14.

Perrin, Noel. 1978. *First Person Rural: Essays of a Sometime Farmer*. Boston: Godine.

———. 1980. *Second Person Rural: More Essays of a Sometime Farmer*. Boston: Godine.

———. 1983. *Third Person Rural: Further Essays of a Sometime Farmer*. Boston: Godine.

———. 1991. *Last Person Rural: Essays*. Boston: D. R. Godine.

Petersen, David, ed. 1996. *A Hunter's Heart: Honest Essays on Blood Sport*. New York: Henry Holt.

Petersen, Thomas Reed, ed. 2006. *A Road Runs Through It: Reviving Wild Places*. Boulder, Colo.: Johnson Books.

Phelps, Almira. 1829. *Familiar Lectures on Botany: Including Practical and Elementary Botany*. New York: H & F. J. Huntington. 1832 edition. Google Books. http://books.google.com/books?id=9WYXAAAAYAAJ.

Picoult, Jodi. 2000. *Plain Truth*. New York: Pocket Books.

Pierce, Naomi, M. F. Braby, A. Heath, D. J. Lohman, J. Mathew, D. B. Rand, and M. A. Travassos. 2002. "The Ecology and Evolution of Ant Association in the Lycaenidae (Lepidoptera)." *Annual Review of Entomology* 47: 733–71.

Pierson, Melissa Holbrook. 2006. *The Place You Love Is Gone: Progress Hits Home*. New York: Norton.

Plum, Sydney Landon. 2007. *Solitary Goose*. Athens: Univ. of Georgia Press.

Pochmann, Ruth Fouts. 1968. *Triple Ridge Farm*. New York: Morrow.

Professional Wildlife Removal. 2007. http://www.wildlife-removal.com /groundhog.htm.

Pyle, Robert Michael. 2007. *Sky Time in Gray's River: Living for Keeps in a Forgotten Place*. Boston: Houghton Mifflin.

Quammen, David. 2008. "Has Success Spoiled the Crow?" In *Natural Acts: A Sidelong View of Science and Nature* (revised and expanded edition), 27–31. New York: Norton.

Ray, Janisse. 2005. *Pinhook: Finding Wholeness in a Fragmented Land*. White River Junction, Vt.: Chelsea Green.

Renfrew, Rosalind. 2008. "Wintering Ecology of Bobolinks." Vermont Center for Ecostudies. http://www.vtecostudies.org/cbd/bobo/index .html.

Rezelman, Jean Doren. 1990. "Early Works on the Finger Lakes Trail." *The Crooked Lake Review*. June. http://crookedlakereview.com/articl es/1_33/27june1990/27rezelman.html.

Rezelman, John. 2010. *Bushels, Barrels, Bags and Boxes: A History of Potato Growing in Steuben County, New York*. Middlebury Center, Penn.: H & H Press.

Rhodes, Richard. 1989. *Farm: A Year in the Life of an American Farmer*. New York: Simon and Schuster.

Rich, Adrienne. 1978. "Transcendental Etude." In *Dreams of a Common Language: Poems, 1974–1977*. 73. New York: Norton.

Rich, Louise Dickinson. 1962. *The Natural World of Louise Dickinson Rich*. New York: Dodd, Mead.

Richards, Dorothy. 1977. *Beaversprite: My Years Building an Animal Sanctuary*. San Francisco: Chronicle Books.

Richards, Jeff. 2007. "A Love for the Land." *Star-Gazette*. Aug. 25.

Richtmyer, Richard. 2008. "Iberdrola Accepts Energy East Buyout Terms." *The Leader*. Sept. 10.

Rogel, Steve. 2003. "Forest Ownership and Forest Responsibility: Weyerhauser Speeches and Interviews." http://www.weyerhauser.com /Company/Media/Speech?dcrID=0121200031.

Rolston, Holmes, III. 1994. *Conserving Natural Values*. New York: Columbia Univ. Press.

Royte, Elizabeth. 2008. *Bottlemania: How Water Went on Sale and Why We Bought It*. New York: Bloomsbury.

Ryden, Hope. 1989. *Lily Pond: Four Years with a Family of Beavers*. New York: Morrow.

Sacks, Oliver. 2002. *Oaxaca Journal*. Washington, D.C.: National Geographic.

Saulny, Susan. 2008. "Timber Thieves Strike at the Heart of Lands Private and Public." *The New York Times*. Jan. 20.

Savage, Candace. 2005. *Crows: Encounters with the Wise Guys*. Vancouver, Canada: Greystone Books.

Scorecard: The Pollution Information Site. 2005. http://www.scorecard .org.

Scott, Jack Denton. 1980. *Window on the Wild*. New York: Putnam.

Shaleshock. 2009. http://www.shaleshock.org.

Sharp, Dallas Lore. 1901. *Wild Life Near Home*. New York: The Century Co.

Small Farm Center: Agritourism. 2008. http://www.sfc.ucdavis.edu /agritourism.

Snow, Dan. 2008. *Listening to Stone*. New York: Artisan Press.

Solnit, Rebecca. 2000. *Wanderlust: A History of Walking*. New York: Penguin.

Spector, Joseph. 2008. "Whistle Blown on Wind Power." *Democrat and Chronicle*. July 28.

Spitzer, Eliot, Frank Partnoy, and William Black. 2009. "Show Us the E-mail." *The New York Times*. Dec. 20, Week in Review, 9.

Staff and Wire Reports. 2008. "Cuomo Announces Wind Farm Ethic Code." *The Leader.* Oct. 31.

Star Gazette. 2010. "Update: Chesapeake Withdraws Pulteney Wastewater Site Plans." Feb. 16.

Steuben County, New York. 1999. "Agricultural Expansion and Development Plan." http://www.steubencony.org/planning/IntoAgPlan.pdf.

The Steuben Courier. 1890. "Country Roads." April 11, *Fry's Local Scrapbook,* vol. 78, 102.

Steuben Spotlight. 2009. Cornell University Cooperative Extension Steuben County Newsletter. vol. 7, issue 4.

Stevens, Kathy. 2009. *Where the Blind Horse Sings: Love and Healing at an Animal Sanctuary.* New York: Skyhorse Publishing.

Stinson, Jim. 2008. "Iberdrola's Dual Roles Big Hurdle." *Democrat and Chronicle.* July 11.

———. 2009. "NYSEG Parent Seeks Rate Increase." *Star-Gazette.* Jan. 30.

Stinson, K. A., S. A. Campbell, J. R. Powell, B. E. Wolfe, R. M. Callaway, G. C. Thelen, S. G. Hallett, D. Prati, and J. N. Klironomos. 2006. "Invasive Plant Suppresses the Growth of Native Tree Seedlings by Disrupting Below-ground Mutalism." *PLoS Biology* 4, no. 5. http://plosbiology.org/articleinfo:doi/10.1371/journal.pbio.0040140.

Stone, Ruth. 2002. "A Woodchuck Lesson." In *The Next Galaxy.* Port Townsend, Wash.: Copper Canyon Press.

Stone Wall Initiative. 2008. http://www.stonewall.uconn.edu.

Sumi, Lisa. 2008. "Shale Gas: Focus on the Marcellus Shale. A Report on Oil and Gas Accountability Project." *Earthworks Report.* May. http://www.earthworks.org/files/publications/OGAPMarcellusShaleReport-6-12-08.pdf?pubs/OGAPMarcellusShaleReport-6-12-08.pdf.

Suzuki, David, Wayne Grady, and Robert Bateman. 2004. *Tree: A Life Story.* Vancouver, Canada: Greystone Books.

Swain, Roger. 1991. "Horse Chestnuts." In *Saving Graces,* 3–6. Boston: Little, Brown.

Swander. Mary. 1995. *Out of This World: A Journey of Healing.* Iowa City: Univ. Iowa Press.

Tautz, Jurgen. 2008. *The Buzz about Bees: Biology of a Superorganism.* Berlin, Germany: Springer-Verlag.

Thomas, Dylan. 1954. *A Child's Christmas in Wales*. New York: New Directions.

Thoreau, Henry David. 1862. *Walking*. Published as *On Walking*. 1924. Girard, Kans.: Haldeman-Julius Co.

Thorson, Robert. 2002. *Stone by Stone: The Magnificent History of New England Stone Walls*. New York: Walker and Company.

Treichler, Martha, and William Treichler. 2007. *Stories of Mt. Washington: Steuben County, New York*. Hammondsport, N.Y.: Crooked Lake Review Books.

Treichler, Rachel. 2006. "Biographical Profile for Rachel Treichler: Candidate for Attorney General." http://www.vote-ny.org/intro.aspx?state=ny&id=nytreichlerrachel.

———. 2008. Rachel Treichler's Blog. http://www.greencommons.org/blog/618.

Treichler, William. 1990. "The Finger Lakes Trail System." *The Crooked Lake Review*. June issue. http://crookedlakereview.com/articles/1_33/27june1990/27treichler2.html.

———. 2004. "Bill Treichler Remembers Balck Mountain College." http://www.bmcprojects.org/MEMOIRS/TREICHLERwilliamMEMOIR.htm.

TRIP. 2005. "Fatalities on Rural Roads." http://www.tripnet.org/national/RuralRoadsPRO30305.htm.

Triumpho, Richard. 2005. *Wait 'Til the Cows Come Home: Farm Country Rambles with a New York Dairyman*. Syracuse: Syracuse Univ. Press.

Trondsen, Jim. 2008. "Bad Things Happen to Good Lakes." Outdoor Forum at http://canaaninstitute.org/bikeski/viewtopic.php?p=765&sid=d4d8e4df1de7af245d51fbd16d8a94de.

Turner, Dorie. 2008. "Ga. Drifter Now Suspect in Fla. Case." *The Leader*. Jan. 10.

Underhill, Linda. 1999. *The Unequal Hours: Moments of Being in the Natural World*. Athens, Ga.: Univ. of Georgia Press.

———. 2009. *The Way of the Woods: Journeys through American Forests*. Corvallis, Ore.: Oregon State Univ. Press.

Unti, Bernard. 2004. *Protecting All Animals: A Fifty-Year History of the Humane Society of the United States*. Washington, D.C.: Humane Society Press.

U.S. Committee on Energy and Commerce. 2007. *Summary of Policy Provisions of the Energy Policy Act of 2005 Conference Report*. http:// abma.com/members/Summary_by_Title_by_House_Energy_Dems .pdf.

U.S. Department of Agriculture. 2008. "Conservation Programs." http:// www.fsa/usda.gov/FSA/webapp?area+home&subject=copr&topic =crp.

————. 2011. Natural Resource Conservation Service. Wildlife Habitat Incentive Program (WHIP). http://www.ny.nres.usda.gov/programs /whip.

U.S. Department of Transportation. 2005. National Center for Statistics and Analysis. Fatality Analysis Reporting System. http://www.nrd .nhtsa.dot/gov/Pubs/809855.pdf.

U.S. News and World Report. 2007. "Why You Should Worry about Water: How This Diminishing Resource Will Determine the Future of Where and How We Live." June 4, 44.

Vasiliev, Ren. 2004. *From Abbotts to Zurich: New York State Placenames*. Syracuse: Syracuse Univ. Press.

Wachman, Richard. 2009. "Guy Hands Moves to Guernsey to Join Tax Exiles." Guardian.co.uk. http://www.guardian.co.uk/business/2009 /may/10/hands-guernsey-tax-exile.

Wallace, Alison. 2006. *A Keeper of Bees: Notes on Hive and Home*. New York: Random House.

Wallace, David Rains. 1980. *Idle Weeds: The Life of a Sandstone Ridge*. San Francisco: Sierra Club Books.

Watts, May Theilgaard. 1957. "Canyon Story or Following a Stream in Southern Indiana." In *Reading the Landscape: An Adventure in Ecology*. 86–108. New York: Macmillan.

Whitman, Walt. 1860. *Song of the Open Road*. From *Leaves of Grass*. The Walt Whitman Archive: U.S. editions of *Leaves of Grass*. http://www .waltwhitmanarchive.org/published/LG.

Whynot, Douglas. 1991. *Following the Bloom: Across America with the Migratory Beekeepers*. Boston: Beacon Press.

Wilber, Tom. 2009. "Cornell Team Concludes DEC Ill-Equipped to Oversee Natural Gas Drilling." *Ithaca Journal*. Dec. 11.

Williams, Alex. 2007. "Water, Water, Everywhere, But Guilt by the Bottle-ful." *New York Times.* Aug. 12.

Wilmer, Caissa. 2004. "Volunteer Profile: A Special Sort of People." *The Land Steward: Newsletter of the Finger Lakes Land Trust* 16, no. 2: 4.

Wilson, Larry. 2008. "Steuben Kidnapping Baffles Police." *Star-Gazette.* Jan. 10.

Winkelman, Babe. 2008. "Conservation Conference Offers Ideas for the 21st Century." *The Courier.* Nov. 16.

Yoder, Don. 2003. *Groundhog Day.* New York: Stackpole Books.

Zacharias, Lee. 2008. "Buzzard." In *The Best American Essays. 2008,* edited by Adam Gopnick, 260–81. Boston: Houghton Mifflin.

Zick, John. 2006. "Three Charged with Arson." *The Leader.* Aug. 20.

———. 2008. "Bath Man Gets 18 Years for Kidnapping." *The Leader.* Oct. 21.

Index

Italic page numbers indicate illustrations.